Shakescenes

four short plays
for Shakespeare lovers

Andrew Wetmore

© 2021 Andrew Wetmore

All rights reserved. No part of this book may be reproduced or transmitted in any form or by any means, electronic or mechanical, including photocopying, or by any information storage or retrieval system, without permission in writing from the publisher.

Cover: Becca Hastings as Sylvie, the actress playing Titania, in "Sprite Fight" at the Saint John Theatre Company in 2015.

ISBN: 978-1-990187-24-7
First edition October, 2021

2475 Perotte Road
Annapolis County, NS
B0S 1A0

moosehousepress.com
info@moosehousepress.com

We live and work in Mi'kma'ki, the ancestral and unceded territory of the Mi'kmaw people. This territory is covered by the "Treaties of Peace and Friendship" which Mi'kmaw and Wolastoqiyik (Maliseet) people first signed with the British Crown in 1725. The treaties did not deal with surrender of lands and resources but in fact recognized Mi'kmaq and Wolastoqiyik (Maliseet) title and established the rules for what was to be an ongoing relationship between nations. We are all Treaty people.

Performance rights

The copyright for the plays in this book belongs to the author. In buying this book you get the enjoyment of putting on the plays in the theatre inside your head, as you read them.

If you want to perform these scripts in any way, including as staged readings for a non-paying audience, as an audio play, or as an amateur or professional live or recorded production, you **must** obtain permission in writing from the author. To do otherwise is a violation of copyright and not a nice thing to do to another theatre person.

For information about royalties and obtaining performance rights, send an email to **info@moosehousepress.com**. We will forward serious inquiries to the author.

About the plays

The best grade I got as an undergrad at McGill University in Montreal was for a rewrite of that classic Greek-comedy play, Plautus' *Mostellaria* (The Haunted House). Tricky servants, ghosts, a superstitious master, a debt, close calls all around...it is one of the source plays for the classic movie *A Funny Thing Happened on the Way to the Forum*.

But the funny thing to me was that the ending sucked. It was like Plautus ran out of time to finish the play in a reasonable way, so there is a miracle ending and everyone is happy. I think my version is way better, but of course, given that *Funny Thing* has pretty much taken the improve-Greek-comedy territory, it has never seen a production.

The plays you hold in your hand, however, have been a bit more fortunate. They are also knock-offs, this time of the works of William Shakespeare.

In 1993 the Hampshire Shakespeare Company, based in Amherst, Massachusetts, had an ambitious script by Brian Marsh: *Lear Solo*, a one-man presentation of *King Lear*. It ran to about an hour, so they asked me and another (more prestigious) playwright if we could come up with short works based on a couple of Shakespeare plays that are less well-known, to fill out the evening. The other playwright was to create a short script based on *Titus Andronicus*, and I drew *Timon of Athens*.

I had never read *Timon of Athens* before. I sped through it, making frantic notes, as I only had a few days to come up with the script. The further I read, the more I understood why you didn't see too many productions of the play these days.

But still, there were plenty of raisins in the suet. I had no trouble putting together a script that would showcase some of the good lines, keep the audience from getting lost or bored, and still do something interesting by the end. In that last point, this Shakespeare script sort of reminded me of the Plautus play.

I turned in "Twenty-Minute Tragedy" in good time, and things went pretty well at the reading. I love it when actors, who have seen it all and have had to act the most dreary stuff, bark a laugh of surprise in the middle of a table reading of a new script.

But at the end of the reading, as the actors were leaving, one of the Hampshire Shakespeare folks drew me aside. There was a problem.

My mood dove for my shoes, but then bounced up again when I understood what the problem was. The other playwright had turned in a script for *Titus Andronicus* that was "too much" for a theatre that had folks of all ages in the audience. They needed a second option, and quickly. Could I possibly turn my hand to a second script? Within a week?

I knew *Titus* a bit better than I had *Timon*, but the process was much the same: a wild gallop through the script, with copious note-taking and counting on my fingers over and over to see how many actors we would need.

I really didn't know what the cast would think of "Loosely Titus". If I remember correctly, they had not seen it before we gathered for a read-through. I was pacing even before they began.

And the laughs started coming right away. The cast could see the potential for visual gags, ways of reading the lines that would deliver a jolt of pleasure to even the hardest-of-hearing audience member.

Now, when I say "the cast", I have been referring to a half-dozen Hampshire Shakespeare regulars. We had four or five actors in the room, the producers, and the director. But each of my plays called for eight warm bodies.

Fortunately, I had a solution to hand. I was at the time the director of Varsity Drama, an after-school theatre program at the Belchertown High School. Those kids were enthusiastic, inventive, and anxious to perform. I was able to recruit three of them to play 'also starring' roles in both plays.

Hampshire Shakespeare produced its plays at that time in the courtyard of the Lord Jeffrey Inn in Amherst, weather permitting. The shows went well, with only one rain-out that I remember, and I think that each evening we set the audience up well to appreciate the more serious and rich material of *Lear Solo*.

I should add that for the kids of Varsity Drama, it was a significant experience. One of them wrote me recently, almost thirty years after the event, to tell me how the group at the school, and especially getting to perform in a 'real' play, changed his life and his sense of himself.

A few years later the good folks at Hampshire Shakespeare asked if I had any more Shakespeare-connected plays. I wrote "Sprite Fight" for them; its inspiration was largely the backstage dramas at Hampshire Shakespeare performances in the courtyard of that Amherst inn.

Unfortunately, the play did not match what the group was looking for. The script had a couple of staged readings in New England, and finally had its premiere with the Saint John Theatre Company in New Brunswick in 2015. I had the great fun of working with the company, and with a dramaturg hired for the event, to get a final polish on what the dramaturg called a "well-oiled machine".

That reminds me, by the by, never to give up on a script. It may find its home and its audience even though the pages of the first copies have long-since turned brittle and yellow.

The newest play, "A Shakespearean Fragment", has not had a full production yet. I would travel quite a long distance to see its premiere. It has had a staged reading in Boston and a couple in smaller locations, so I continue to hope. I wrote this play while thinking about how the influence of Shakespeare pervades, flows far outside formal theatre settings, and structures our very language.

Andrew Wetmore
Clementsport, Nova Scotia
October, 2021

For RHW, who has read an awful lot of shaky first drafts.

These plays are works of fiction. The author has created the characters, conversations, interactions, and events; and any resemblance of any character to any real person is coincidental.

Contents

Performance rights..3
About the plays...5
Cast requirements..13
Twenty-Minute Tragedy..15
Sprite Fight...45
A Shakespearean Fragment...81
Loosely Titus...133
Acknowledgements..163
About the author..165

Andrew Wetmore

Cast requirements

I wrote three of these scripts with a specific acting company in mind, and therefore specified how many men and women we would need. As long as you do not violate the intention of the play, you may opt to fill parts with actors of any gender.

Twenty-Minute Tragedy
Six men
Two women
One offstage voice
Four men play multiple parts

Sprite Fight
Two men
Two women

A Shakespearean Fragment
Four men
Two women

Loosely Titus
Six men
Two women
One woman and one man play multiple parts

Andrew Wetmore

Shakescenes

Twenty-Minute Tragedy

Time
Now, and classical Athens

Setting
Various scenes in classical Athens, including a banquet hall and a wilderness.

Cast
Several actors play multiple parts

M1: Timon of Athens
M2: Flavius
M3: Poet, dinner guest, Lucius, first bandit, crowd member
M4: Painter, dinner guest, Lucullus, second bandit, crowd member
M5: Apemantus, third bandit, crowd member (singing voice)
M6: Alcibiades, Sempronius
W1: Actor playing Timandra, a prostitute
W2: Actor playing Phrynia, a prostitute
Offstage voice: a member of the lighting crew

Script note:
From pages 39 to 41 there are a series of fill-in-the blanks speeches, as in the original production we referred to people our local audience knew. Replace the blanks with references to cast members, local theatres, and famous local actors, as indicated in the parentheses.

15

Andrew Wetmore

The Hampshire Shakespeare Company
presents

Shakespeare Under The Stars
— *in the garden of the* —
Lord Jeffery Inn
— Amherst, Mass. —

As You Like It – June 22-July 10
Directed by Brian Smith

Timon, Titus and Lear – July 13-July 24
Directed by Sarah Wilson

Romeo and Juliet – July 27-August 15
Directed by Julie Dixon

Performances at 8:00 pm
Tuesday (Discount Night), Thursday, Friday & Saturday
Raindates Sunday

Twenty-minute Tragedy

SOUND: Trumpets and drums.
ENTER a POET and a PAINTER.
To one side of the acting area are TIMANDRA and PHRYNIA, wearing headsets.

POET
Good day, sir.

PAINTER
I'm glad you're well.

POET
I have not seen you long. How goes the world?

PAINTER
It wears, sir, as it grows.

POET
Ay, that's well known....
You see how all conditions, how all minds,
As well of glib and slippery creatures as
Of grave and austere quality, tender down
Their services to Lord Timon. His large fortune,
Upon his good and gracious nature hanging,
Subdues and properties to his love and tendance
All sorts of hearts; yea, from the glass-fac'd flatterer
To Apemantus, that few things loves better
Than to abhor himself: even he drops down

The knee before him, and returns in peace
Most rich in Timon's nod.

PAINTER
I saw them speak together...

> *Timandra and Phrynia address the audience. The play goes on in mime behind them.*

TIMANDRA
Do you realize what you've got yourself into—

PHRYNIA
—on your hard seats among, like, total strangers?

TIMANDRA
Nope. You haven't a clue.

PHRYNIA
Just came to see some "classical culture". Your probation officer sent you, right?

TIMANDRA
But these rude mechanicals have no pity. They propose to inflict on you—

PHRYNIA
—unless we can stop them—

TIMANDRA
—that fiduciary tragedy, that saga of a man who was as good as gold, Timon—

PHRYNIA
—or T*ih*mon—

TIMANDRA
—of Athens.

> *ENTER TIMON, FLAVIUS, APEMANTUS and ALCIBIADES. All on stage gather around Timon, laying their cases before him and receiving largesse from him. Only Flavius is aware of the women.*

TIMANDRA
See him in his glory, draped in citizenry, who love to bring their woes to him. Oh, does he have deep, deep pockets. And everybody wants to live in them. He's rich—

PHRYNIA
—and therefore popular—

TIMANDRA
—and generous—

PHRYNIA
—because he's rich.

TIMANDRA
But no brains, no brains.

PHRYNIA
A fool and his money will soon party.

> *Flavius bustles down to them.*

FLAVIUS
What are you doing? You're part of the cast. You're, you're, um—

PHRYNIA
Timandra and Phrynia, the good time girls. In Act 4.

FLAVIUS
But you're not part of the crew.

PHRYNIA
We volunteered to help. They're very nice. They said, Thank you very much, and they gave us these neat t-shirts.

FLAVIUS
You can't distract the audience now. They want to hear the play.

TIMANDRA
They'd rather talk to us.

FLAVIUS
They'll have to wait until Act 4.
(to the audience)
Um, lend us your ears: over there.

TIMON
...Imprisoned is he, say you?

ALCIBIADES
Ay, my good lord. Five talents is his debt,
His means most short, his creditors most strait.
Your honorable letter he desires
To those who have shut him up; which failing him,
Periods his comfort.

TIMON
...Well,
I am not of that feather to shake off
My friend when he must need me. I do know him
A gentleman that well deserves a help,
Which he shall have. I'll pay the debt and free him.

ALCIBIADES
Your lordship ever binds him.

TIMON
Commend me to him: I will send his ransom;
And, being enfranchis'd, bid him come to me—

FLAVIUS
All happiness to your honour!

>*General applause. The men execute a change of scene to the banquet in Timon's house.*

TIMANDRA
(To the audience)
Not on until Act 4!

PHRYNIA
And then we're just prostitutes.

TIMANDRA
Phrynia and Timandra, no better than we ought to be—

PHRYNIA
For about thirty seconds of stage time: two bit hookers.

>*Flavius crosses down to them.*

FLAVIUS
Get off stage. Or else—

TIMANDRA
Or else what? We're part of the crew, sweetie. And you know it's the crew that runs the show.

>*FLAVIUS reaches for her.*

Andrew Wetmore

VOICE
(from the booth)
One more step and you'll never see lights again!

> *Flavius stops, glances up at the light booth; reaches for her again.*

VOICE
No flourishes, no hautboys, no tuckets without.

FLAVIUS
This is piracy!

PHRYNIA
If you had helped put up the set, maybe they'd listen to you, too.

FLAVIUS
We all had a chance to express ourselves during rehearsals.

PHRYNIA
But nobody listened to us girls.

TIMANDRA
(to the audience)
The boys wanted to talk about authorship. I'm up to here with the Earl of Oxford.

PHRYNIA
This is a dumb show.

FLAVIUS
It's Shakespeare!

PHRYNIA
Dumb Shakespeare.

TIMANDRA
He wrote a will that's got more zip than this. Hey—Why don't we put on Will's will?

PHRYNIA
"And to my wife, the second-best bed, with the furniture." That's great stuff.

FLAVIUS
You don't understand.

TIMANDRA
Is this some guy thing?

FLAVIUS
Timon of Athens is about a great man betrayed by a corrupt society. It foreshadows King Lear. It has riveting passages of great power and lyric beauty—

TIMANDRA
Like the prayer of Apemantus?

APEMANTUS
(chant-singing)
Immortal gods, I crave no pelf.
I pray for no man but myself.
Grant I may never prove so fond
To trust a man on his oath or bond.
Or a harlot for her weeping,
Or a dog that seems a-sleeping,
Or a keeper with my freedom,
Or my friends, if I should need 'em.

ALL
(chant-singing)
Amen.

APEMANTUS
So fall to't.
Rich men sin, and I eat root.

The feast begins.

TIMANDRA
"Power and lyric beauty"?

FLAVIUS
Apemantus expresses the spiritual nausea of a worldly age.

TIMANDRA
(to Phrynia)
It's a guy thing.

FLAVIUS
It's not supposed to be frilly-pretty. It's supposed to be a backdrop for Timon. His goodness against their greed.

TIMANDRA
He has no goodness. He's a charge card on legs. He doesn't even know where his money comes from, so it doesn't hurt him to give it away.

PHRYNIA
And he doesn't give it, like, to day-care centres. He just parties.

As the party-goers begin to leave, Timon gives them gifts.

TIMANDRA
You play Flavius, his trusty steward, right?

FLAVIUS
I do.

TIMANDRA
Do you know where his money comes from?

FLAVIUS
Where it comes from doesn't matter!

TIMANDRA and PHRYNIA
(to each other)
It's a guy thing.

FLAVIUS
What matters is he loses it, and then nobody will help him.

> *When all the guests are gone, Timon realizes his pockets are empty.*

FLAVIUS
It's a moral and cautionary tale for this or any age.

TIMANDRA
He's a baby. Who does he blame when he finally figures out he's in trouble? He blames Flavius, his trusty steward.

> *Flavius hustles upstage to Timon.*

TIMON
You make me marvel wherefore ere this time
Had you not fully laid my state before me,
That I might so have rated my expense
As I had leave of means.

Andrew Wetmore

FLAVIUS
You would not hear me.
At many leisures I proposed—

TIMON
Go to!
Perchance some single vantages you took
 when my indisposition put you back,
And that unaptness made your minister
Thus to excuse yourself.

FLAVIUS
(Lear-like, his patience at an end)
O my good lord,
At many times I brought in my accounts,
Laid them before you. You would throw them off
And say you found them in mine honesty.
When for some trifling present you have bid me
Return so much, I have shook my head and wept;
Yea, 'gainst th' authority of manners prayed you
To hold your hand more close. I did endure
Not seldom, nor no slight checks, when I have
Prompted you in the ebb of your estate
And your great flow of debts. My lovèd lord,
Though you hear now too late, yet now's a time;

Hands Timon a sheaf of accounts.

FLAVIUS
The greatest of your having lacks a half
To pay your present debts.

TIMON
Oh. Right.

TIMANDRA
This is your kind, thoughtful, heroic master?

Flavius comes down to them.
EXIT Timon, studying the accounts.

FLAVIUS
It's the style of moral tragedy. Timon doesn't have to be complicated or brilliant; he just stands for goodness. Like in a parable.

TIMANDRA
This is supposed to be a play. If I want a parable—

PHRYNIA
—I'll get me to a nunnery.

TIMANDRA
So what does this good man do when he's deep in debt? Does he go cap-in-hand to the friends he has helped, friends who might now turn him down and humiliate him in his hour of need? No. He makes *Flavius* go cap-in-hand to those who are happy to humiliate him.

ENTER Lucullus, Lucius, and Sempronius, the 'Three Friends'.
They take up pompous positions, like Roman statues.
Flavius approaches Lucullus.

LUCULLUS
Thy lord's a bountiful gentleman; but thou art wise, and thou know'st well enough, although thou com'st to me, that this is not time to lend money especially upon bare friendship, without security.

Flavius approaches Lucius.

LUCIUS
Commend me bountifully to his good lordship, and I hope his honour will conceive the fairest of me, because I have no power to be kind. And tell him this from me: I count it one of my greatest afflictions, say, that I cannot pleasure such an honourable gentleman.

Flavius approaches Sempronius.

SEMPRONIUS
Must I be his last refuge? His friends, like physicians,
Thrive, give him over. Must I take th' cure upon me?
I'd rather than the worth of thrice the sum
He'd sent to me first, but for my mind's sake;
I'd such a courage to do him good. But now return,
And with your faint reply this answer join:
Who bates mine honour shall not know my coin.

Flavius comes down to the women as the Three Friends set up the feast.
   ENTER Timon with covered dishes.

FLAVIUS
But even you have to admire this great man's defiant gesture, in the face of disdain and rejection. He invites his false friends to one last, grand banquet in the mansion he must leave.

PHRYNIA
Oh, sure, I like this bit.

TIMON
Each man to his stool, with that spur as he would to the lip of his mistress. Make not a city feast of it, to let the meat cool ere we can agree upon the first place; sit, sit.

The Three Friends sit and reach for the food.

TIMON
The gods require our thanks.

They withdraw their hands and bow their heads piously.

TIMON
You great benefactors, sprinkle our society with thankfulness...
Make the meat be beloved more than the man that gives it. Let no assembly of twenty be without a score of villains. If there sit twelve women at the table, let a dozen of them be—as they are.

TIMANDRA
That's it. He's toast.

Flavius restrains her.
Thinking the grace is over, the Three Friends raise their heads.

TIMON
For these my present friends,

They hurriedly bow their heads again.

TIMON
As they are to me nothing, so in nothing bless them, and to nothing are they welcome. Uncover, dogs, and lap!

The Three Friends uncover the dishes and look in.

SEMPRONIUS
This is naught but water.

LUCULLUS
What does his lordship mean?

Andrew Wetmore

LUCIUS
I know not.

TIMON
May you a better feast never behold,
You knot of mouth-friends! Smoke and lukewarm water
Is your perfection. This is Timon's last,
Who, stuck and spangled with your flatteries,
Washes it off and sprinkles in your faces
Your reeking villainy.

> *He throws the water in their faces, then administers a slapstick beating on them.*

TIMON
Live loathed and long,
Most smiling, smooth, detested parasites,
Courteous destroyers, affable wolves, meek bears,
You fools of fortune, trencher-friends, time's flies,
Cap-and-knee slaves, vapors, and minute-jacks!
Of man and beast the infinite malady
Crust you quite o'er! What, dost thou go?
Soft! Take thy physic first! Thou too, and thou!

> *They dodge and cower.*

TIMON
What, all in motion? Henceforth be no feast
Whereat a villain's not a welcome guest.
Burn, house! Sink, Athens! Henceforth hated be
Of Timon, man, and all humanity!

> *He EXITS.*

LUCULLUS
How now, my lords?

LUCIUS
Push! Did you see my cap?

SEMPRONIUS
He's but a mad lord, and naught but humors sways him. He gave me a jewel th'other day, and now he has beat it out of my hat. Did you see my jewel?

LUCIUS
Did you see my cap?

LUCULLUS
Here 'tis.

SEMPRONIUS
Let's make no stay. Lord Timon's mad. I feel 't upon my bones.

ALL THREE
One day he gives us diamonds, next day stones.

The Three Friends EXIT with the banquet table.

TIMANDRA
Big deal. I've done that at lots of parties.

FLAVIUS
Why are you acting like this? Some of these people are paying customers! What do you want? What's so wrong with this play?

PHRYNIA
Oh, so finally he asks.

FLAVIUS
I've been asking you—

PHRYNIA
Have not. You've been telling us.

TIMANDRA
It's your thing, guy.

FLAVIUS
Come on: Timon falls from wealth and grace, and falls from a romantic belief in the goodness of man, to a bleak, postmodernist assessment of the failures of all men's strivings.

> *ENTER Timon in rags. He scrabbles at the ground, looking for food.*

FLAVIUS
That's right up your alley, Timandra.

TIMANDRA
Watch it.

FLAVIUS
He hates all humanity, becomes a hermit grubbing for roots to eat, and finishes his life in curses and misanthropy. I can't see why lovely ladies such as yourselves wouldn't adore this play.

PHRYNIA
You still don't know? Watch. We'll be right back...

> *EXIT Phrynia and Timandra.*

TIMON
Earth, yield me roots!
Who seek for better of thee, sauce his palate
With thy most operant poison!

> *He finds some small, heavy bags.*

TIMON
What is here? Gold? Yellow, glittering, precious gold?

FLAVIUS
(helpfully, to the audience)
Somebody else's buried treasure.

PHRYNIA
(Pokes her head out from off-stage)
Shh!

TIMON
No, gods, I am no idle votarist.
Roots, you clear heavens! Thus much of this will make
Black white, foul fair, wrong right,
Base noble, old young, coward valiant.
Ha, you gods! Why this? What this, you gods? Why, this
Will lug your priests and servants from your sides,
Pluck stout men's pillows from below their heads
This yellow slave

> *ENTER Alcibiades, with Timandra and Phrynia, in some guy's idea of sexy clothing, on his arms. (Phrynia's T-shirt is concealed somewhere.) They approach Timon.*

TIMON
Will knit and break religions, bless th'accurst,
Make the hoar leprosy adored, place thieves
And give them title, knee, and approbation
With senators on the bench. This is it—

ALCIBIADES
Noble Timon, what friendship may I do thee?

> *He offers Phrynia to him. She writhes seductively around him.*

TIMON
This fell whore of thine
Hath in her more destruction than thy sword,
For all her cherubin look.

PHRYNIA
Thy lips rot off!

TIMON
(to Alcibiades)
Promise me friendship, but perform none.
If thou wilt not promise, the gods plague thee, for thou art a man!
If thou dost perform, confound thee, for thou art a man!

TIMANDRA
Is this th'Athenian minion whom the world
Voiced so regardfully?

TIMON
Art thou Timandra?

TIMANDRA
Yes.

TIMON
Be a whore still. They love thee not that use thee;
Give them diseases, leaving with thee their lust...

TIMANDRA
Hang thee, monster!

She tries to hit him. Alcibiades restrains her.

ALCIBIADES
Why, fare thee well. Here is some gold for thee.

TIMON
Keep it. I cannot eat it.
 Put up thy gold. Go on

He shows the gold he found.

TIMON
Here's gold—go on.

PHRYNIA and TIMANDRA
Give us some gold, good Timon. Hast thou more?

TIMON
Enough to make a whore forswear her trade.
Hold up, you sluts, your aprons mountant—

He gives them a sack of gold each.

PHRYNIA
Well, more gold. What then?

TIMANDRA
Believe't that we'll do anything for gold.

TIMON
Consumptions sow
 In hollow bones of man; strike their sharp shins
and mar men's spurring...
Paint till a horse may mire upon your face.
A pox of wrinkles!

PHRYNIA and TIMANDRA
More counsel with more money, bounteous Timon.

TIMON throws a bag of money toward Flavius and the women follow it. Alcibiades EXITS. Timon returns to

> *grubbing. Phrynia puts her T-shirt back on.*

TIMANDRA
What's wrong is, the guy cannot write women's parts.

PHRYNIA It's politically incorrect.

TIMANDRA
It's an anti-women play.

FLAVIUS
It's an anti-everybody play. That's what's I love about it.

> *He gestures at the stage.*
> *ENTER THREE BANDITTI, who surround Timon and threaten him in grotesque pantomime style.*

FLAVIUS
Even the bandits are bad bandits.

FIRST BANDIT
(threateningly)
We are not thieves,

SECOND BANDIT
(menacingly)
But men that much do want.

THIRD BANDIT
(at a loss for words)
Ummm...Aarggh!!

TIMON
Rascal thieves.
Here's gold.

He throws down little bags of gold. The banditti wrestle over them.

TIMON
Go, suck the subtle blood o' the grape
Till the high fever seethe your blood to froth,
And so scape hanging....
Do villainy, do, since you protest to do 't,
Like workmen. I'll example you with thievery.
The sun's a thief, and with his great attraction
Robs the vast sea. The moon's an arrant thief,
And her pale fire she snatches from the sun.
The sea's a thief, whose liquid surge resolves
The moon into salt tears. The earth's a thief,
That feeds and breeds by a composture stolen
 From general excrement. Each thing's a thief.
The laws, your curb and whip, in their rough power
Has unchecked theft. Love not yourselves. Away!
Rob one another. There's more gold.

He throws it.

TIMON
Cut throats.
All that you meet are thieves. To Athens go.
Break open shops; nothing can you steal
But thieves do lose it. Steal less for this I give you,
And gold confound you howsoe'er! Amen.

He throws down more bags of gold and EXITS, grubbing for food.

THIRD BANDIT
He's almost charmed me from my profession by persuading me to it.

Andrew Wetmore

FIRST BANDIT
I'll believe him as an enemy, and give over my trade.

SECOND BANDIT
Let us first see peace in Athens. There is no time so miserable but a man may be true.

EXEUNT.

FLAVIUS
(At full soliloquy pitch)
O you gods!
Is yon despised and ruinous man my lord?

PHRYNIA
You big phony!

FLAVIUS
(breaking character)
What?

PHRYNIA
You don't believe any of the hot air you've been blowing by us. You just like this play because you get a lot of good lines.

FLAVIUS
Not at all. A loyal steward never thinks of himself.

PHRYNIA
That's what you want them
(the audience)
to go home thinking.
(to Timandra)
He thinks the play's about him!

FLAVIUS
You've got to understand. Parts like this are my only hope. I'm not compelling like _____ (name of actor playing Timon), I don't have _____'s looks (name of actor playing Alcibiades), and I can't sing like _____ (name of actor playing Apemantus) can. And I hate the bit parts.

PHRYNIA
Amen to that.

FLAVIUS
So I live for parts like this. Not too big, so the stars will grab it, not too small to have fun with. And maybe the audience will go home remembering me.

TIMANDRA
Stick with me, kid, and I'll make you a star.

  Phrynia EXITS.

FLAVIUS
What?

TIMANDRA
We have a plan to save the play.

FLAVIUS
You'll let the play go on? You'll let me do my lines? What plan?

TIMANDRA
Well, we're just girls, and it's probably not a good plan...

FLAVIUS
It's a great plan: I'm for it! What is it?

  Timandra strides up into the playing area. The Three

Andrew Wetmore

> *Friends, Apemantus, and Alcibiades enter and listen as she takes up Timon's lines.*

TIMANDRA
I have a tree, which grows here in my close,
That mine own use invites me to cut down,
And shortly must I fell it. Tell my friends,
Tell Athens, in the sequence of degree
From high to low throughout, that whoso please
To stop affliction, let him take his haste,
Come hither ere my tree hath felt the ax,
And hang himself. I pray you, do my greeting.

> *Her audience reacts in grief and EXITS in sorrow.*

FLAVIUS
What—what are you doing?

TIMANDRA
Simone of Athens.

FLAVIUS
"Simone of Athens"?

TIMANDRA
It's a perfect solution! The cruelty of the friends, the feast of water, the hatred of rotten mankind—it all plays great if Timon is Simone!

FLAVIUS
You can't do that—!

TIMANDRA
The crew loves it.

FLAVIUS
(after a glance at the light booth.)
I mean...We already have it cast. _____ (Name of actor playing Timon) is playing Timon.

Phrynia ENTERS.

PHRYNIA
All settled.

FLAVIUS
What's all settled?

PHRYNIA
_____(name of actor playing Timon) is settled. I told him poor _____(famous local actor) is trying to do *King Lear* all by himself, so he volunteered to quit this cast and go help. He always wanted to play the fool.

FLAVIUS
But—but—

PHRYNIA
It's okay: _____ (name of actor playing Timon) doesn't mind. He says this play has too many roots and not enough sword fights.

FLAVIUS
But _____ (famous local actor) doesn't need him!

PHRYNIA
That's his problem.

TIMANDRA
Don't despair, _____ (Name of actor playing Flavius). You haven't lost a Timon; you've gained a Simone.

FLAVIUS
(of Phrynia)
But what about her? What part does she want?

PHRYNIA
I don't want nothin'. I'm staying with the crew. They have better parties.

TIMANDRA
So it's all up to you. Do we boycott this woman-hating, slime-spewing Elizabethan disaster, and you don't get to do your lines? Or do we move on to a daring, provocative, insightful Simone of Athens?

> *A beat. Then Flavius decides. He strides up onto the acting area and strikes an oratorical pose. Timandra goes up onto the acting area and lies down on what was the banquet table.*
> *The rest of the cast ENTERS and becomes pallbearers ready to bear Timandra off.*

FLAVIUS
Here lies a wretched corpse, of wretched soul bereft. Seek not her name. A plague consume you wicked caitiffs left!

TIMANDRA
Here lie I, Simone, who, alive, all living men did hate. Pass by and curse thy fill, but pass and stay not here thy gait.

PHRYNIA
(to audience)
These well express in her her latter spirits.

FLAVIUS
Though thou abhorredst in us our human griefs,
Scornedst our brains' flow and those our droplets which

From niggard nature fall, yet rich conceit
Taught thee to make vast Neptune weep for aye
On thy low grave, on faults forgiven. Dead
Is noble Simone—

PHRYNIA
Of whose memory
Hereafter more.

TIMANDRA
[As they lift her up, cortege-style, onto their shoulders and begin to carry her off.]
Bring me into your city,
And I will use the olive with my sword,
Make war breed peace, make peace stint war, make each
Prescribe to other as each other's leech.

PHRYNIA
(Into headset)
Let our drums strike!

> *Flourish of trumpets and drums.*
> *EXEUNT.*

Blackout.

End.

Andrew Wetmore

Sprite Fight

Time
A summer evening

Setting
The dressing tent backstage at an outdoors production of *Midsummer Night's Dream*. Costumes, a makeup table with mirrors, Bottom's donkey head, and other paraphernalia spread about over folding tables and chairs. The stage is OL,

Cast

Jessie: Director of the play

Ted: The producer

Sylvie: A starlet; has been playing Titania

Mr Bothwell: Father of a cast member, in a three-piece suit

Andrew Wetmore

Sprite Fight

The dressing tent of a summer theatre production of "A Midsummer Night's Dream". The stage is OL, for that is where APPLAUSE is coming from at the rise. It is evidently the final curtain call.

JESSIE, the director of the play, and TED, the producer, are standing in the middle of the tent, looking OL. As the applause dies down, they look at each other.

JESSIE
Okay, are you satisfied?

TED
No.

JESSIE
I've missed the curtain call of *Midsummer Night's Dream*. The director misses the curtain call. On opening night.

TED
Some things are more important than even a curtain call.

JESSIE
So you're going to make me miss the buffet reception, too? Will that satisfy you?

TED
It's not about—

JESSIE
The cast is going to need this tent. They need to change.

TED
We have to settle this first.

JESSIE
There's nothing to settle.

TED
There is if you want to have a second night to go with your opening night.

JESSIE
I wonder if Shakespeare had problems like this.

TED
So you agree there's a problem!

JESSIE
It's a nothing! An incident...an event...a blooper...a--

TED
Where you have blood, you have a problem. That's a rule.

JESSIE
I'm the director, you're the producer.

TED
You create the problems and I get to solve them? No way.

JESSIE
Okay, next time I'll be the producer—

TED
There won't *be* a next time if we don't sort this out. Got it? Now, they'll be in here any second—

JESSIE
This is why we have liability insurance.

TED
It covers fire, flood, and bad critical reviews. It does not cover violent assault. Or blood. I checked.

JESSIE
It's got to cover blood! This is the theatre!

TED
Not blood gushing out because of violent assault. Jessie, we are talking criminal code here. Civil suit.

JESSIE
Okay. Okay. What do we have to do?

TED
It will probably include sincere listening and groveling.

JESSIE
(Indiana Jones impersonation)
Sincerity? I hate sincerity, Jock!

TED
But you do it so well.

JESSIE
Why should I be the one who has to grovel? You stroke the stage mothers till they purr.

TED
This is a stage father.

JESSIE
Oh, hell. Well, where is he?

TED
I sent Albert to go find him.

JESSIE
And where's the kid with the bloody nose?

TED
Chantal insisted on taking her curtain call. With a bloody handkerchief held to her face. I asked Sylvie to feed her cake until we're done.

JESSIE
You asked Sylvie to take care of the kid. And Sylvie will do about anything you ask.

Unconsciously they start moving closer to each other.

TED
I don't know what you mean.

JESSIE
Uh-huh.

TED
Come on: she's a good actress. She's doing Titania just fine.

JESSIE
She's terrible. I don't know what Oberon sees in her. I hope she's better with you than she is with him.

TED
It's nothing like that at all!

JESSIE
It's something worse?

TED
Jessie. We agreed that our ending our relationship wasn't going to spill over into our theatre work.

JESSIE
Did I say anything about our former relationship?

TED
What we had...Sylvie and I have nothing like that.

JESSIE
I'll take that as a compliment.

TED
There is nothing between me and Sylvie.

JESSIE
Just skin on skin, huh?

TED
You do catty so well.

JESSIE
You drive me to it. I'm just vitriol in your hands.

They are now very close to each other.

JESSIE
Sir, I believe you are well inside my personal space.

Andrew Wetmore

TED
This is a bad thing?

JESSIE
Without permission? Yes.

TED
I'm in my own personal space, too.

JESSIE
My personal space was here first.

TED
Egad, it was. Could I, perhaps, just overlay your space with my space?

JESSIE
Like before? No way, buster.

TED
Parts of before were really good.

JESSIE
I don't want parts. I want all. Can you give me all?

TED
Well...

JESSIE
What about Sylvie?

TED
Oh, that's just a theatre thing.

JESSIE
Just like last time, then. Back off, space man.

Ted steps back two paces.

JESSIE
Now where's the other kid, the one who punched this one?

TED
Jasmine. She's at the reception with her family, I guess.

JESSIE
Do they know?

TED
How many parents do you want to deal with at one time?

JESSIE
I don't deal with my own parents. Why should I deal with anybody else's parents?

TED
And: the child Jasmine hit? Her name is Chantal.

JESSIE
So what?

TED
Try to remember it. That will show that you care.

JESSIE
I don't care. Who in his right mind would care about a swarm of little ankle-biters who can't take direction, can't hold character, can't sing, can't move, can't hold still, can't remember their lines, can't be heard when they do remember them, and take potty breaks on-stage?

Andrew Wetmore

TED
They're our actors of the future—

JESSIE
It's not the kids who are stage-struck: it's their parents. Half those kids don't even know what a stage is. They have the attention span of canaries and the social graces of rats. This is Shakespeare. It's hard enough already without having kids in the cast.

TED
It was a good idea.

JESSIE
In the next show, we could have sprite gravediggers. Sprite courtiers. We could do *Hamlet of Oz*.
(Munchkin voice for the courtier, normal voice for Hamlet)
"My lord, I think I saw him yesternight."
"Saw? Who?"
"My lord, the king your father."
"The king my father?"
"Season your admiration for a while, With an attent ear, till Dorothy can explain it in a song."

TED
Look at the box office. We are ninety percent sold. That has never happened before, even when you put that nude scene in *MacBeth*.

JESSIE
Now *that* was a good idea. And it's a lucky thing we didn't have sprites bouncing about in that show.
(Munchkin voice, with Scottish accent.)
"Och, aye: Ah can see yon MacBeth's wee slickit sporran."

TED
We're not in New York any more, Jessie. This is community theatre. You don't sell community theatre tickets with a thirty-second nude

scene.

JESSIE
It should have been longer?

TED
You sell tickets with sprites. Tens of little tiny actors, making their little tiny entrances and exits and doing their little tiny dance around Titania's bower. Every one of them comes attached to tens of great big relatives who buy tickets. Who bring their friends and buy tickets for them. The parents of their classmates buy tickets.

JESSIE
I am a classically-trained actor.

TED
Nobody is saying—

JESSIE
I am a director with more awards than you've had hot suppers. And now I have to share my stage with sprites? I have put my whole heart into this business.

TED
And this is where it got you.

> *Beat.*

JESSIE
Thanks a lot.

TED
What I mean—

JESSIE
I am good. I am. And I work harder than anybody. But you need

luck as well as training and heart. You need luck.

TED
And sometimes you need sprites.

JESSIE
I don't need sprites!

TED
A couple more shows with ticket sales like this, sprite-fed ticket sales, and we'll be back out of debt.

JESSIE
Us? Out of debt?

TED
And then...no more tiny actors.

JESSIE
You promise?

TED
We can go cold-spritey.

JESSIE
No more debt...then we could try some shows that are not Shakespeare. Some real, new theatre...

TED
Jessie, this is what got us in trouble before.

JESSIE
Then why do we even try? What's the point of all this sweat and sorrow, if all we're allowed to do is safe theatre?

TED
We're theatre people. Do you think we have a choice about doing theatre? Does a snake have a choice about slithering?

JESSIE
I could quit.

TED
And do...what, exactly?

Beat. Jessie considers a life without theatre.

JESSIE
Crap.

TED
But don't lose heart. Fixing impossible problems is part of the theatre thing.

JESSIE
Okay. Okay. Couple more shows with ankle-biters. But after that: better scripts, Ted!

TED
Jessie—

JESSIE
"Tempest" next year: has to be, for the damn sprites.

TED
We have to sort out this blood bath first. Or there will be no more shows of any kind.

JESSIE
Arrgh. Okay. So I have to grovel. Is it a single parent?

TED
Divorced.

JESSIE
So I can touch his arm sympathetically. Should I bat my eyes?

TED
How many lawsuits do you want at one time?

> *SYLVIE ENTERS, wearing the costume of Titania, the fairy queen.*

SYLVIE
Ta-dah! So, what did you think? Not bad for a first-time fairy queen, right?

TED
Sylvie—

SYLVIE
You see, Jessie? Ted was right to get you to cast me.
   The audience loved me—the show, I mean. It's not a bad script, although we could fix some of the words—

TED
Sylvie, where is Chantal?

SYLVIE
I mean, why do I have to say "bower"? Who gets "bower"? Why can't I just say "bedroom"?

JESSIE
When you said "bower", I'm sure they heard "bedroom."

SYLVIE
I hope so. I hope so. I sort of leaned over and did that thing with my cleavage like Ted suggested.

JESSIE
That thing with your cleavage?

SYLVIE
We worked on it for hours. You want to see it?

TED
Where is Chantal?

SYLVIE
Out there, of course.

TED
You were supposed to be watching her.

SYLVIE
I *was* watching her. And I gave her cake, like you said, and told her what a brave little sprite she was, and got her some punch to wash the cake down with, and after a few glasses she put her head down on the table and went to sleep.

TED
Fell asleep? The punch you gave her—do you mean you gave her some of the punch meant for grownups? Or do you mean some of the equally-attractive-but-non-alcoholic punch from the bowl on the kids' table?

SYLVIE
There's a kids' table?

TED
Oh, Sylvie...you got her drunk?

SYLVIE
Not too much.

JESSIE
And you left her alone?

SYLVIE
No, her dad's with her. And Albert. They were trying to wake her up.

TED
Maybe we could just change our names and move to New Zealand.

 Ted EXITS L.

SYLVIE
So, anyway, Jessie, I had this great idea.

JESSIE
You did.

SYLVIE
And it really fits in with how you are always trying to get better parts for women.

JESSIE
Does this great idea involve sprites?

SYLVIE
Aren't they cute? I loved the way they were all arguing in their little mouse voices about how to handle Bottom's ass.

JESSIE
They were what?

SYLVIE
(Crossing to the donkey head)
It's a big crisis for the sprites. In the scene when he's lying in my lap with his ass-head on, and they're supposed to be fondling his ears and everything? Well, according to the sprites, if you touch the ears you get boy cooties, but if you touch the nose right after, you get okay again.

JESSIE
Boy cooties?

SYLVIE
Yeah. Like:
(touching an ear)
"Eeuwh."
(touching the nose)
"I'm a princess again."
(touching an ear)
"Eeuwh."

JESSIE
This is what they're talking about? Onstage? During the show?

SYLVIE
It's so cute. There's Titania getting it on with Bottom, rubbing cooties all over herself, and they're dancing all around the bower, worried about his ears.

JESSIE
They're supposed to be thinking about their parts!

SYLVIE
Oh, come on, Jessie. You know what actors think about. They're thinking, "Did I smear my lipstick on that last kiss, and is my downstage foot back far enough, and omigod, there's Tara and Biff sitting together in the third row—I'm so glad they came to see

me...I'm so pissed they came to see me together." Why should the sprites be any different?

JESSIE
That's not what I think about when I'm acting!
SYLVIE
Well, we can't all rise to your level, Jessie. Now, about my idea...

> *Remembers that she touched the ear last on the donkey head. Half-embarrassed, goes back and touches the nose.*

SYLVIE
I just love being in this show, and I just love being Titania, the Queen of Chiffon. But there are limits to being gorgeous and sexy, you know? Always with the guy and the cleavage and the giggle—you know how it is.

JESSIE
No.

SYLVIE
And I've been thinking there's got to be more to acting then being drop-dead gorgeous, right?

JESSIE
Right.

SYLVIE
So, while I was offstage tonight—and have you noticed that Titania is offstage a *lot*?—I started thinking wouldn't it be neat to double?

JESSIE
You want to play two parts?

SYLVIE
All the big actors do it. You know, so you can play one character

type-cast, and one character really, really different. Like in my case that would be on the type-cast side Titania: beautiful and sexy. So I got to thinking, who would be on the other side? Who would make me really stretch, but it has to be somebody that I'm not in a scene with, because that would be almost impossible, right?

JESSIE
Almost.

SYLVIE
And I suddenly realized, there's a super character I am never in a scene with in this whole play.

JESSIE
Sometimes they double Titania and Hippolyta. But Alice is playing Hippolyta.

SYLVIE
Not Hippolyta! She's just the duke's trophy wife: boring.

JESSIE
Okay, then.

SYLVIE
I want for the other character one that would really stretch my theatre talents: Caliban!

JESSIE
Caliban?

SYLVIE
Caliban: Prospero's slave! I know he's normally a guy, but I thought it would be really edgy—the kind of thing you really like—to have a girl play him: "This island's mine, by Sycorax my mother, which thou tak'st from me." Wouldn't that be cool? Wicked cool?

JESSIE
The reason Titania is never in a scene with Caliban—

SYLVIE
Ooh—maybe Shakespeare meant the parts to be doubled! What a guy, that Shakespeare.

JESSIE
Caliban is in "The Tempest". This is "Midsummer Night's Dream".

SYLVIE
Are you sure? So who am I thinking of?

JESSIE
God only knows.

SYLVIE
Wow. Boy, that's really too bad, because I've been really working on what I would do with Caliban, you know? Like, how would I make him different from Titania?

JESSIE
That would be a challenge.

SYLVIE
Yeah. But I came up with something I thought you would like. It's really sort of based on this guy I saw in a music video.

JESSIE
Sylvie, you don't have to do this.

SYLVIE
I put a lot of work into it. Besides, you didn't get to see the cleavage thing.

Sylvie takes on Caliban character. This involves a fair bit of gorilla-like grunting and posturing.

JESSIE
All right, then. "Thou poisonous slave, got by the devil himself upon thy wicked dam, come forth!"

SYLVIE
(breaking character)
What?

JESSIE
Act 1, Scene 2. That's what Prospero says to Caliban. It's called a "cue".

SYLVIE
Oh, I thought that was you....Okay, give it to me again.

Takes on Caliban character. Then breaks character to say:

SYLVIE
Oh, listen: I do like this sort of character-establishing thing before I speak, so when I do that, that's what I'm doing.

JESSIE
Oh.

SYLVIE
Because I know the lines.

JESSIE
Are you ready?

SYLVIE takes on her Caliban character.

Andrew Wetmore

JESSIE
"Thou poisonous slave, got by the devil himself upon thy wicked dam, come forth!"

> *SYLVIE's cave-man vocalizations are somewhere between a deep grunt and a cough.*
> *TED and MR. BOTHWELL ENTER.*

TED
She's choking!

> *He leaps forward and grabs Sylvie around the middle from behind.*

JESSIE
No, she's okay!

TED
Heimlich maneuver!

JESSIE
No, don't!

TED
Clear!

> *Ted tries to squeeze Sophie, who emits a wet squawk.*

TED
Again!

JESSIE
No! She's okay!

TED
So soon?

SYLVIE
(breathless)
She is.

Ted releases her, and she sits down suddenly.

SYLVIE
Ow.

JESSIE
Her hero.

TED
Well, *you* weren't doing anything.

JESSIE
Because she wasn't choking.

TED
She wasn't?

JESSIE
She was auditioning. For Caliban.

TED
Are you out of your mind?

JESSIE
Soon, if not now.

TED
She can't play Caliban.

SYLVIE
Yes, I can.

Andrew Wetmore

TED
I see what you're up to, Jessie. You're trying to make a fool of her. You're trying to make her look stupid and shallow and completely untalented.

SYLVIE
Hey!

TED
If we're doing "The Tempest" next year, there's only one part for Sylvie, and that's Miranda.

SYLVIE
(standing)
I want to audition for—

TED
It's perfect for her: Miranda is sweet and innocent and inexperienced and gullible, and she doesn't have to do much except fall for Ferdinand. It's type-cast for Sylvie!

SYLVIE
Oh! Oh, you, you—dumb guy.

TED
You don't understand—

SYLVIE
I understand. "Inexperienced and gullible"---I understand. Well, I'm going to audition for Caliban. I don't care what you say. And don't you ever touch my Heimlich again.

    Sylvie EXITS.

TED
What did I say?

JESSIE
You always act before you think.

TED
I was just trying to—

JESSIE
Make things worse?

TED
I better go talk to her.

JESSIE
After we settle the sprite thing.

TED
Oh, my gosh, yes! Jessie, you remember Mr. Bothwell.

JESSIE
Ah, Mr. Bothwell, of course!

TED
But I've got to tell you—

JESSIE
Just let me handle this.

TED
But I've got to tell you—

JESSIE
Not a word!

TED
Just as you say.

JESSIE shakes hands with Bothwell.

JESSIE
You've been to one or two of the rehearsals.

BOTHWELL
I've been to all of them.

JESSIE
We are very impressed with your daughter…

TED
Chantal.

JESSIE
Chantal.

BOTHWELL
She loves the theatre. Always has. That's why I so deeply regret today's events.

JESSIE
And so do I, Mr. Bothwell.

BOTHWELL
I did a little theatre in my college days. And I always thought, you know, if I had only taken that road less travelled by, where would I be today and what would I be doing?

JESSIE
But I'm sure the road you took—

BOTHWELL
I might be backstage somewhere at this very moment.

JESSIE
You are: you're backstage here.

BOTHWELL
Why, so I am. I'm backstage here.

He gazes around.

BOTHWELL
Well, well...well. It must be more exciting if you're actually *in* the play...

JESSIE
Oh, yes.

BOTHWELL
That's the experience I want my Chantal to have. Before she has to choose a career and join the real world.

JESSIE
Mr. Bothwell, I assure you: we set out to provide an exciting theatre experience for every child, for every cast member. An exciting, safe experience—

BOTHWELL
But it wouldn't really be theatre if it was entirely safe, would it?

He laughs; Jessie and Ted laugh along with him.

JESSIE
We try to keep it just this side of the shedding of, er, blood.

BOTHWELL
(earnest)
My daughter is distraught.

Andrew Wetmore

JESSIE
Oh, I'm sure.

BOTHWELL
The tension of the performance, and then this sad incident—why, she's sleeping in a chair out there, in the midst of the reception! I can't wake her up.

JESSIE
She put a lot of energy into her performance. Dear...

TED
Chantal.

JESSIE
Chantal.

BOTHWELL
Now, my point is this: I want it absolutely clear there will not be a repetition of this incident.

JESSIE
Absolutely. I assure you—

BOTHWELL
In this day and age, we cannot have loose blood flying around.

JESSIE
Certainly not.

BOTHWELL
And of course I would undertake to have every single costume dry-cleaned.

JESSIE
(after a moment)
You would what?

BOTHWELL
Or replaced, if you think that would be better. To remove any possible trace of blood.

JESSIE
You think we have to replace the costumes?

BOTHWELL
You and Ted will be the judges, of course. But I do not want anything to stand in the way of Chantal continuing in this play. How much should I make the cheque out for?

JESSIE
Uh...

TED
May I explain?

JESSIE
Can you?

TED
Once Mr. Bothwell heard the sequence of events from Albert, who was right there in the bower with the sprites, he was very concerned about your reaction.

JESSIE
My reaction.

TED
That you would come down hard on Chantal.

JESSIE
Wait. She's the one with the—

TED
Chantal and Jasmine were in some sort of dispute in Titania's bower—

JESSIE
Oh, the cooties.

BOTHWELL
"The cooties"?

JESSIE
Theatre jargon.

TED
And Chantal fell victim to her histrionic vehemence.

JESSIE
You mean Jasmine.

TED
I mean Chantal, Mr. Bothwell's daughter.

BOTHWELL
My daughter, yes.

JESSIE
Chantal. The one with the bloody—

TED
Season your admiration for a while, With an attent ear, till I may deliver. Behold: I am Jasmine; Mr. Bothwell is Chantal.

BOTHWELL
Oh: I'm playing a part.

>*He mimes as Ted speaks.*

TED
Yes. So: Chantal made a fist and went to bop Jasmine one, as a way of emphasizing her side of the argument...

BOTHWELL
Oh, it's me: And Jasmine brought up her arms to defend herself...

>*Ted crosses his arms in front of his face.*

TED
And Chantal's fist hit Jasmine's arms, and bounced right back into Chantal's own nose.

>*Bothwell mimes this and tries to mime the reactions as Ted names them.*

TED
Astonishment...chagrin...blood...tears.

JESSIE
Amazing.

TED
You can see where Chantal gets her talent.

BOTHWELL
I'm sure that, after a good night's sleep, Chantal will understand that, er, bopping other cast members is not the best way to get the dramatic point across. I will speak with her about it. Her mother will speak with her about it. Oh, lord: her mother will speak with *me* about it.

JESSIE
Mr. Bothwell—

BOTHWELL
We will pray about it.

JESSIE
I don't know what to say.

TED
Five hundred dollars for the dry cleaning and new costumes, and we give Chantal another chance.

JESSIE
Five hundred—!

BOTHWELL
I agree that sounds quite low. Are you sure that will be enough?

TED
You are very astute. I believe we could make it happen for an even thousand.

BOTHWELL
(patting his pockets)
My chequebook? Oh, it must be in my topcoat pocket. I left it on my chair, with my umbrella and my blanket. I will be right back.

> *He starts to leave; returns and pumps Jessie's hand and then Ted's.*

BOTHWELL
I cannot thank you enough. All Chantal needs is a second chance. God bless you, every one.

> *Bothwell EXITS.*

JESSIE
I don't understand.

TED
The magic of theatre. Disaster averted by means nobody quite understands, and an extra thousand dollars in the bank!

JESSIE
The problem went away? It's done?

TED
Sans teeth, sans eyes, sans taste, sans everything.

JESSIE
You made that happen, Ted, and I didn't even see how.

TED
The show can go on. And the next show, and the next show—

JESSIE
Bring your personal space over here.

TED
Really? Well, I seem to be available...

JESSIE
I suddenly need one of your Heimlichs.

They embrace. Sylvie ENTERS and sees them.

SYLVIE
The sprites were right!

TED and JESSIE jump apart.

SYLVIE
Telling each other in the bower about you two, what they saw. All about you two looking at each other, touching....And I didn't believe them. You two are nasty, conniving, back-behind-going theatre people! You can get yourself another Titania.

JESSIE
He probably will.

TED
Sylvie, wait.

SYLVIE
Oh, I almost forgot. Jasmine's father is outside.

TED
That's Chantal's father.

JESSIE
The bloody one.

SYLVIE
You think I don't know a thing. Chantal's dad is the cute worried guy with the umbrella. Jasmine's dad is the big angry guy.

JESSIE
The big angry guy.

SYLVIE
He wants to talk to who's in charge. Jasmine's mother took Jasmine to the hospital.

TED
The hospital.

SYLVIE
They think she has a broken wrist. How would she get a broken wrist in a play, her dad wants to know. He wants to have a word with who's in charge. Who is in charge?

TED	JESSIE
Uh...	Well...

SYLVIE
Good luck, then.

SYLVIE EXITS. TED and JESSIE stare at each other.

TED	JESSIE
You deal with this one!	You deal with this one!

BLACKOUT
END

Andrew Wetmore

A Shakespearean Fragment

Time
Now.

Setting
A city restaurant in the middle of the afternoon. Tables, with four chairs each, DR, DL and UC. UL, the counter and kitchen; UR, the exit. DL, the way to the washrooms.

   The DR table has, as a centrepiece, a spray of artificial flowers of some sort. The DL table has an artificial rose. The UC table does not have a vase.

Cast

DOYLE: A waitress in her thirties

JOHN: An enforcer in a dark suit and sunglasses

HANNUM: A man of substance in a good suit and topcoat

TAVERNER: A 'deal-maker.' A thin man in a seedy jacket

MRS. NOVOTNY: A substantial woman of a certain age

MORASH: Professorial, near-sighted, timid

Andrew Wetmore

A Shakespearean Fragment

>*DOYLE, a waitress, skids among the tables of a shabby restaurant, looking for tips, blowing salt off the edge of tables, eating a cracker abandoned on a plate. She picks up empty dishes.*

DOYLE
(Calling OL)
No, sit down, sit down! Don't be such a hero. If you ignore a back spasm it might turn into something really serious. My Aunt Jane had terrible back spasms, for I don't know how long, and she just tried to ignore them, and it turned out she was going to have a baby! So you just take care of yourself, or you don't know what might happen.

>*JOHN ENTERS R. He is in a suit and raincoat, with grey gloves. He stands just inside the entrance, looking around.*

DOYLE
We've got nothing to worry about until the supper rush, anyway. So you just put your feet up, or your head between your knees, or whatever it takes, and let your back take care of—

>*She notices John.*

DOYLE
Oh. Oh, hello. I'm sorry. was just—well, you know. Bellowing isn't

normally part of the ambience, but I didn't think anybody was here. Sit anywhere you like—are you by yourself?

John crosses L to look into the kitchen.

DOYLE
Usually nobody comes in here in the afternoons, so that's why I didn't expect you—well, not *you* exactly, but anyone. I don't even know why they keep the place open in the afternoons—blind faith, I guess.
    That's the kitchen—no seating in there. Well, we can, but you can't. That's my partner, Betty—hi, Betty! Feeling any better? She's sitting down because of her back. I don't know where Lou is; he's the chef, but he's mostly asleep at this time of day. No, your sitting choices are out here. Any table you want.

JOHN crosses DC, surveys the rest of the room, where the audience is.

DOYLE
I can't even say smoking or non-smoking anymore. Well, I could *say* it, but the smoking section is out in the alley, and we can't even keep a chair out there to sit on because people keep stealing them. So what would be the point of saying—?

JOHN
(Gesturing DL)
What's through there?

DOYLE
Well, the men's room if you want it, the ladies', of course, and the place for the mops. Why?

JOHN
Is there a exit?

DOYLE
It's *an* exit, and no, there is not. If you want to leave, you have to go the way you came. Or go through the kitchen and out into the alley. The way I came. Where I come from, you always got to leave by the door where you came in, or it's bad luck. My uncle Fletcher—

JOHN
(Indicating the table DR)
We'll sit here.

DOYLE
I'm sorry, I've got to work.

JOHN
What?

DOYLE
What? Oh—I thought you meant *you and me*. Sit here. I mean, that would be awfully sudden, but the way you said it—

JOHN
Party of four. Coffee. Four cups and a carafe. Milk, not cream. Cube sugar. Basket of bread sticks.

DOYLE
All right. Do you—?

JOHN
And nothing else unless we call for you.

DOYLE
"Please, ma'am. If it's not too much trouble, ma'am."

JOHN
Now.

DOYLE
You can catch a lot more flies with honey—

JOHN
If I ever want flies, I'll ask your advice.

> *After a moment, Doyle pushes her jaw closed with one hand, turns, and marches to the service table, UL. Crashes some silverware onto a tray, and brings it down to the chosen table. John has moved UR, standing between the exit and the table nearest to it.*

DOYLE
You've changed your mind? You want to sit over there?

JOHN
No.

DOYLE
Okay. You want a long straw, so you can drink your coffee from there?

JOHN
I don't drink coffee.

DOYLE
O-kay.

> *Sets the table*

DOYLE
I have this neighbour who says poopy behaviour in grownups is directly related to their potty training, and another neighbour who puts it all down to astrological signs. In which case you must be a crab or a bull. What do you put it down to?

JOHN
I hate restaurants. Too many things go wrong in them.

DOYLE
Well, I'm with you there. Work in a kitchen long enough, and you want to eat home all the rest of your life.

> *She crosses to him*

DOYLE
I'd be careful of the breadsticks. You don't know where they've been.

> *She EXITS L.*

JOHN
(under his breath)
You don't watch out, girl, you'll find 'em stuck where you don't want 'em.

> *Doyle ENTERS with cups and coffee stuff on a tray, but no carafe.*

DOYLE
We don't normally do a carafe. I put on a fresh pot of coffee just now. We're happy to come refill your cup for no extra charge.

JOHN
If you want your tip, you'll keep your distance.

DOYLE
(setting the table)
Life is more than tips.

Andrew Wetmore

JOHN
Not for you.

DOYLE
There are more things between heaven and earth, my dear Horatio, than your tough-guy stuff is aware of.

JOHN
What?

DOYLE
I'll just get the carafe.

> *She EXITS L.*

JOHN
My name's John. Who's this Horatio guy? Hey?

> *As he stands facing L, HANNUM ENTERS R. He is wearing a good suit and an elegant topcoat. Stands looking at JOHN.*

JOHN
Well, say something!

HANNUM
(Softly)
Bang.

> *John leaps into the air, scrabbles for his gun, turns, stumbles against the table, and ends up lying across it with the gun on the floor.*

Hannum
I am so glad you are my bodyguard, John. You boost my confidence.

JOHN
(Scrambling up, collecting his gun.)
Sorry, Mr. Hannum. I'm very sorry. I was just checking out the kitchen.

HANNUM
It's all right, John.

JOHN
I mean, there's an alley entrance. There should really be another guy, or two guys—

HANNUM
It's all right.

JOHN
I can't watch everything at the same time.

HANNUM
Put that thing away and listen.

> *JOHN holsters gun.*

HANNUM
These are just salesmen, amateurs. All you will need to do is protect my image as a dominant, powerful person who is not to be fooled with: so no more falling down, all right?

JOHN
Yes, Mr. Hannum, no.

HANNUM
Now: where are we sitting?

JOHN
(Gestures DR)
I thought, over there, sir.

HANNUM
(Gesturing DL)
Not over there?

JOHN
No, sir. Too close to the washroom doors. You never know what might pop out of a place like that.

HANNUM
All right. Good.

> *He crosses DR and inspects the table. He caresses the artificial flowers that are the centrepiece, holding a stem for a moment. Then crosses L and sits at that table. Notices JOHN staring.*

HANNUM
Should you not be watching the door?

> *JOHN starts to respond; stifles himself and turns toward the door R.*
> *DOYLE ENTERS with carafe, places it on DR table and crosses to HANNUM.*

DOYLE
Well, hello. I didn't hear you come in. This is getting to be a busy afternoon. Would you like a menu?

HANNUM
I'm with him.

DOYLE
You are? Why?

HANNUM
Our fates are not in the stars, but in ourselves.

DOYLE
Well, that's for sure. Do you want me to move everything over here?

HANNUM
No. I do not expect to be here long.

DOYLE
All right. Anything you want.

Crosses UC to hiss at John.

DOYLE
Manners, breeding: that's more like it.

JOHN
(Turning to look at her)
What?

DOYLE
Pay attention!

EXITS L
As JOHN turns back R, THREE PEOPLE ENTER. They are TAVERNER, a thin man in a seedy jacket; MRS. NOVOTNY, a substantial woman with a grip on Taverner's arm; and MORASH, an older, near-sighted man with a briefcase who trails the others.

JOHN
Ah! I mean, are you—?

TAVERNER
Taverner. Larry Taverner. My associates and I have an appointment here with—

JOHN
Keep your voice down! You want the whole world to know?

TAVERNER
Ah.
(to the other two)
See, these guys are pros.
(to JOHN)
Well, good. That's great. Yup. Is he here?

JOHN
See if you can pick him out from the crowd.

TAVERNER
Oh. Right.
(Suddenly nervous)
Ah-hah, ah-hah.

    Novotny shakes his arm.

TAVERNER
Ahem. Okay. You two wait here, while I just...

    Slips his arm out of Novotny's grasp and, attempting to appear casual, crosses to Hannum.

MORASH
(To Novotny)
So these are professionals. The big leagues. Well, I never would

have dreamed...Are they going to frisk us?

NOVOTNY
(To John)
Are you going to frisk us?

JOHN
It's, um, not necessary.

NOVOTNY
Pity.
(To Morash)
No.

MORASH
Oh, good. Because I am particularly ticklish under the...well, I guess it doesn't matter.

TAVERNER
Mr. Hannum? Nice to meet you, after all the phone calls.

HANNUM
Delightful.

TAVERNER
So. My colleagues and I...You want to sit here, huh?

HANNUM
I am sitting here.

TAVERNER
Yes.

> *Looks closely at the rose in the vase, then at Hannum, then back at the rose.*

TAVERNER
It's just that, of all the silk flowers I am not fond of roses. They tend to harbour bugs...

> *He reaches for the centerpiece. Hannum snakes out his hand and grasps Taverner's wrist.*

HANNUM
I would like the rose to stay right here.

TAVERNER
Ah-hah. Ah-hah. Well, good. Let it stay.

> *Hannum releases his wrist.*

TAVERNER
But, um, let me invite you to *our* table over there.

> *Crosses to the DR table.*

TAVERNER
(To his colleagues)
Come on, come on: here is just the place for us. Clean and bug-free.

> *Novotny and Morash join him.*

TAVERNER
Yes, yes. And look: here's coffee waiting for us! What a restaurant!

> *He pours coffee into cups.*

MORASH
Is there tea of any kind?

NOVOTNY
Coffee is required for this sort of deal. Or something stronger.

MORASH
Oh.

NOVOTNY
You do not need to drink it. Just stir it idly with your spoon to show you are at ease.

MORASH
Spoon. Stir. Right.

TAVERNER
(Under his breath)
I think he has a microphone in the rose over there. That's why I'm making him come over here.

MORASH
My goodness. I never would have thought—

TAVERNER
That's why I'm here: you need an expert for a job like this. Take a seat, sit down. Let him come to us.

> *They sit, leaving the DR chair at their table unoccupied. Then they turn as one and look at Hannum. He stares back.*
> *After a moment Doyle ENTERS with bread sticks and a plate of croissants.*

DOYLE
These croy-sants are just warm from the oven, so I thought I'd bring them along, too.

> *Stops C, taking in the scene.*

DOYLE
Huh. Are we all on one check?

HANNUM
We are.

DOYLE
O-kay. I could leave these here on the floor...

HANNUM
No, it's all right. I am joining them at that table.

TAVERNER
(to his colleagues)
One point for us!

DOYLE
Okey-dokie.

> *She crosses to table DR and sets food on it. Morash reaches for a croissant, but Novotony stops him with a glare. Doyle hefts the carafe.*

DOYLE
Well, that didn't last you long. I'll just go get some fresh.

> *She swings up past John, who waves her along. She signs that he is nuts. She EXITS L.*
>   *HANNUM rises, crosses leisurely to the table R. The others watch him, then swivel around to see where JOHN is. JOHN tries to look tough and professional. The three swivel back to HANNUM, watching him as he crosses behind them and stops with his hand on the empty DR chair. The three, not taking their eyes off HANNUM, pick up their spoons and simultaneously start stirring their coffee, clattering the spoons on the insides of the cups.*

HANNUM
No coffee for me. I find it makes me too tense.

The three stop stirring, Morash continuing longest.

HANNUM
You are Mr. Taverner, of course.

TAVERNER
Yes, yes, I am. And it's a great pleasure to meet you at last.

He rises, takes Hannum's hand in both of his and pumps vigorously.

HANNUM
Your hands are sweaty and cold.

Taverner releases him; rubs his own hands together.

TAVERNER
Oh, no. No, they're not. It's just the condensation from the outside of the carafe. Cold by contrast. Yes.

HANNUM
And these are your associates.

TAVERNER
Well, yours also, I hope. Um, may I present Mr. Morash, the possessor of the fragment. And Mrs. Novotny.

HANNUM
I was expecting Mr. Morash. I know your reputation, sir.

MORASH
(Simpering)
Oh, my.

Andrew Wetmore

HANNUM
But you, Mrs. Novotny, are a new element.

He sits. Taverner hastily sits.

HANNUM
Could I learn what your part in this is?

TAVERNER
She is a friend of mine, a good and generous friend. She has a great interest in antiquities.

MORASH
(to Novotny) You do?

TAVERNER
Oh, it's well-known. Well-known. A great interest.

HANNUM
But what is your interest in this particular antiquity? Are you interested in bidding on it against me?

TAVERNER
A great *academic* interest, I should say. A *theoretical* interest.

NOVOTNY
I have no interest in antiquities.

TAVERNER
Mrs. Novotny, you promised.

NOVOTNY
He is speaking right to me. It would be rude to not answer.

Doyle ENTERS with carafe, crosses to the table

HANNUM
And what did you promise?

NOVOTNY
That I could watch and listen, but I was to keep my mouth shut.

HANNUM
Mr. Taverner, know this: all who are at table with me, are welcome to speak.

DOYLE
(Setting down carafe)
Well, if that's the case, let me just say we are pulling some lovely fresh-fruit pies out of the oven. A piece of pie, maybe with a little ice cream on top, would go very well with your coffee.

TAVERNER
No. Thank you.

MORASH
What kinds do you have?

TAVERNER
We don't want any!

DOYLE
Fine, then. I just thought I'd mention it.

HANNUM
Thank you.

DOYLE
Thank *you*.

Andrew Wetmore

> *She EXITS to kitchen, exchanging gestures with JOHN as she goes.*

HANNUM
Mrs. Novotny, you are absolved of your promise of silence. I would very much like to know why you are here.

TAVERNER
Does it really matter?

NOVOTNY
It is simple like this. Mr. Taverner owes me some money. I believe that he brings you and Mr. Morash together to do some business, and that for his efforts somebody is going to pay him a, a—

HANNUM
A finder's fee.

NOVOTNY
Yes: exactly. A finding fee. He assures me that this fee will be more than what he owes me.

TAVERNER
It would, if we could just get on with this deal.

NOVOTNY
But—how to put it?—Mr. Taverner has many claims on his money. I do not want one of those other claims to find his finding fee before he has the chance to pay me.

HANNUM
I see.

NOVOTNY
I am sorry to intrude. I do not want to be here—no offence intended.

HANNUM
None taken.

NOVOTNY
And now I will say no more and you can get on with your little business.

> *She pats Taverner's hand and then folds her hands on the table in front of her.*

TAVERNER
(To Hannum)
I am very sorry for this—you know how it is.

HANNUM
I do now. Rest assured, Mrs. Novotny, that once this deal is concluded, Mr. Taverner will be in funds.

TAVERNER
Well. That's great, then.
(rubbing his hands.)
I knew this was going to work out great.

HANNUM
Mr. Morash,—

TAVERNER
This is first-rate, quality material. You won't be sorry.

HANNUM
No. Mr. Morash,—

TAVERNER
Everybody knows he's a collector with an unimpreach—, with a perfect reputation for—

Andrew Wetmore

HANNUM
(Forcefully)
Mr. Morash.
(Normal tone)
I have looked into your career and I know of your collection. Very impressive.

MORASH
Oh, no. Oh, no. It is just an old man's hobby.

HANNUM
More than that.

MORASH
My parents left me the means, and after that silly business at the university I no longer cared to teach. So I look for this or that. Sometimes I find it. When I find it, I buy it.

TAVERNER
You should see his apartment! Cases and cases of—

HANNUM
Enough!

Taverner shrinks back. Hannum addresses Morash.

Hannum
There are many desperate people, like your associate, driven by real needs to extreme measures. If he has been in your apartment, and assessed its treasures, you will need to revise your security measures.

MORASH
Oh, well, I—

HANNUM
John?

JOHN
(crossing to the table)
Yes, sir?

HANNUM
Mr. Morash, this is John. He works for me. If you wish, he can visit you and advise about your doors and windows and motion detectors.

MORASH
Motion detectors? Oh, my.

TAVERNER
Hey, wait a minute. What are you saying?

HANNUM
That Mr. Morash needs to review his security—

TAVERNER
You said because of me.

HANNUM
As you say.

TAVERNER
I'm no thief! I'm an entrepreneur, a venture capitalist. Without me, you two wouldn't even—

John puts his hands on Taverner's shoulders.

JOHN
I hear a loud, rude noise. Should I take it out to the alley?

Andrew Wetmore

HANNUM
No, no. If he is quiet, he can stay.

JOHN
He'll be quiet.

> *He removes his hands. Taverner rubs his shoulders.*

HANNUM
Thank you, John.

> *John retreats upstage.*

Hannum
Is there a theme to your collection?

MORASH
Mere curiosity. I'm a magpie. I hear of some special thing, perhaps something nobody had seen for a long time, and I begin to think I would like to see it. And I look and look until I find it. I saw the coat Lord Nelson wore at the Battle of Trafalgar, when he was shot, and I thought, this museum has the bullet hole, but who has the bullet?

HANNUM
And?

MORASH
(Simpering)
I have the bullet now. I have feathers from the last passenger pigeon. I have Patrick Henry's blindfold.

HANNUM
Admirable.

NOVOTNY
but what do you do with feathers? With an old bullet?

(to Hannum)
Sorry.

MORASH
Do with them? They draw me, and I cherish them. Who knows why? I started at this too late to know why. I preserve the things that draw me. When they draw me no longer, I get rid of them. When that silly movie came out, I dumped all my "Titanic" pieces right away.

TAVERNER
You what?

MORASH
That movie made them feel cheap to me. So I sold them to a scrap dealer. He gave me a reasonable price, considering the rust.

TAVERNER
A scrap dealer...You could have made millions.

HANNUM
You are missing the point—

TAVERNER
No, *you guys* are missing the point. You are missing the whole point. Why struggle and spend and sweat to get that stuff, just to throw it away? That's not how it's supposed to work.

NOVOTNY
But the things are his—

TAVERNER
No, they aren't! Nothing is anybody's. It's just passing through your fingers. Even if you put your money in your mattress and lie on it until you die, it's going to go to somebody else. Nothing is anybody's.

MORASH
It feels like it's mine.

TAVERNER
It's just visiting. It's supposed to move on—from you to her, from her to him. That's commerce. The flow of stuff. To and from people, money trading hands for stuff, stuff going for money. That's what it's all about.

HANNUM
That is one interpre—

TAVERNER
That's what it's all about. And that's where I come in. Entrepreneurs like me. Matching money and stuff, stuff and money, helping it pass back and forth.

HANNUM
And scraping off for yourself a bit of everything that goes through your hands.

TAVERNER
Right! You've got it! That's what it's all about. Without that trade, where would I be?
(to MORASH)
Do you understand now? When you throw stuff out in the garbage, you're killing me.

MORASH
Oh, dear.

HANNUM
I think you should be grateful to Mr. Morash. Each artifact he throws away, after all, makes the others more valuable. Rarity drives up price.

TAVERNER
So, like, I have two Fabergé eggs, and I should crush one so the other one will be worth more than twice as much? Uh, uh. No, no. You can't count on that. As soon as you crush one, the Fabergé Bunny comes along and lays six more and the bottom falls out of the market. No, no. It's about constant flow, stuff going in, money coming out.
(to MORASH)
Please don't mess with it. I don't want to starve!

Doyle ENTERS with tray of pie servings.

DOYLE
I thought you would change your mind.

JOHN
Oh, no!

DOYLE
Nobody starves in this restaurant!

JOHN
We will if we want to.

DOYLE
(Crossing to the table)
Don't be silly. Now, we have three different kinds—

As she lifts a serving off the tray, John seizes her around the waist to haul her away. As they struggle, both the serving in her right hand and the full tray in her left inadvertently threaten the people around the table.

DOYLE
Hey! Stop that!

JOHN
Come on, you.

DOYLE
I have a job to do!

JOHN
So do I!

HANNUM
John!

They freeze in place, Doyle on one foot.

HANNUM
John: this is not elegant. This coat is made of...?

JOHN
Uh, virgin wool.

HANNUM
And that pie is...?

DOYLE
(she has to look)
Cherry, it's cherry. But there's also—

HANNUM
This is not elegant, John. I foresee a disaster if you continue struggling, a disaster that will involve a large cleaning bill that will come out of your paycheck.

JOHN
I...don't know what to do.

DOYLE
For starters, you can get your thumb off my underwire.

He releases her.

DOYLE
Ow.

HANNUM
John, the elegant way would have been to shoot her before she got near the table.

DOYLE
What?

HANNUM
As long as you caught the tray before it fell. Since she has reached the table, the elegant thing to do would be to relieve her of the tray...

John does so.

HANNUM
Set it down on the table...

John does so.

HANNUM
And bring her a chair to sit on.

JOHN
With you?

HANNUM
She seems so anxious to join us.

JOHN brings a chair

HANNUM
You have a name, ma'am?

DOYLE
Doyle. That's my first name. D-o-l-l: Doyle.

HANNUM
Sit down, Doyle.

She does, still holding the pie serving.

HANNUM
(To Taverner)
Now, then, sir. She is not one of my staff. Is she part of some plan of yours to complicate this purchase?

TAVERNER
I never saw her before! I was never in this restaurant before! This is a straight-up deal. If we could ever get to it.

HANNUM
All right then, Doyle. For whom do you work?

DOYLE
For the restaurant. And I clean houses three mornings a week.

Notices serving of pie in her hand; offers it.

DOYLE
I was just doing my job.

MORASH
Cherry, you said?

HANNUM
Mr. Morash, be my guest.

MORASH takes the pie, starts to eat with his coffee spoon.

HANNUM
Doyle, I'm afraid I do not believe you. John, you will have to search her for microphones and weapons.

TAVERNER
You think she's a fed?

HANNUM
I thought you said this was a straight-up sale.

TAVERNER
It is. It is.

HANNUM
Then we have nothing to fear from the government. I was thinking more of other collectors. My rivals.

JOHN
(His hands on DOYLE's shoulders)
Search her here, or out back?

HANNUM
Here will be fine.

NOVOTNY
Can you do that?

HANNUM
Probably not. But John can.

Andrew Wetmore

DOYLE
I just work for the restaurant!

HANNUM
John?

John lifts her by the shoulders.

DOYLE
Wait, wait, wait. Okay, okay. I'll tell you why I keep coming out here.

HANNUM
Good.

DOYLE
I don't know what you people are up to, and I really don't care. I don't know who you are, and I hope I never see you again.
(to JOHN)
Especially you.
(to HANNUM)
But I got to get out of the kitchen.
(to John) You met Betty, right?
(to HANNUM)
Betty, that's the other waitress today, she's got a bad back. He saw her: she had her feet up, I'm doing her tables. This is one. Well, we've got this cook—he's new. He said he had a way of dealing with her back pain, and she said okay, anything is better than this, and, fine, he started with her feet. But things have been progressing, and they are getting to know each other really well, and her mind is not on her back right now although she herself is, if you follow me, and three's a crowd, right? So my choice is stand in the alley or come in here.
(to MORASH)
They didn't go anywhere near the pies, so you're fine.

MORASH
(Dismayed)
Oh!
(Then comforted)
Oh.

He reaches for a piece of pie off the tray.

NOVOTNY
Where is the owner?

DOYLE
He'll be along for the dinner crowd. But they'll be done by then.

TAVERNER
But we probably won't.

HANNUM
Mr. Taverner is correct. Doyle, we cannot have you coming and going like this if we are to conclude our business. But I sympathize with your plight. Unless other customers come in, please stay here and stay mute.

TAVERNER
Oh, come on—!

HANNUM
Do you want to conclude this transaction or do you not?
(To Doyle)
John, here, will stay by your side. If I have to, I will ask him to escort you out. I hope I will not have to.

DOYLE
Oh, no. Oh, no.

HANNUM
Good. Have some pie.
(To Taverner)
Unless, of course, you have a strong objection. The resolution of which will take even more time.

TAVERNER
Oh, all right. She can stay. But I draw the line at the cook. He has to find his own deal.

NOVOTNY
He already did.

MORASH
This is very good. Do you bake every day?

DOYLE
Fresh every day.
(taking a serving)
I don't usually get any but the leftovers.
(to NOVOTNY)
And if you were thinking of saying something smart about the cook, forget it.

TAVERNER
Can we please do what we came here for?

HANNUM
Certainly.

He takes a piece of pie. Novotny follows his lead.

Hannum
Doyle, we are concluding a business transaction. Mr. Morash owns a rare object, and I wish to buy it for my collection. You have heard of William Shakespeare?

DOYLE
Sure. He wrote those plays you have to study in school.

HANNUM
We have all studied them or seen them, and our heads are full of what he wrote: "To be or not to be..."

NOVOTNY
"Something's rotten in Denmark."

TAVERNER
"A pound of flesh."

All look at John.

JOHN
(After a moment)
"Red sky at morning, sailors take warning." Yeah, I know who he is.

MORASH
(reaching for more pie)
I am tired of Shakespeare. I have his best bed, I have the Globe Theatre fire-drill procedures—enough is enough.

HANNUM
Mr. Morash also has an artifact in Shakespeare's own hand. This is very rare, Doyle. We have a few William Shakespeare signatures, some legal documents—but no plays, nothing of significance in his own hand. All those plays you studied in school were copies of copies of copies, printed and reprinted over three hundred years. We had thought that the originals were long gone—fallen to dust, destroyed by fire. But Mr. Morash has something in Shakespeare's own hand—

MORASH
Oh, wait—

HANNUM
—and to possess that, I am willing to pay a very high amount. Yes, Mr. Morash?

MORASH
Well, but I—a very high amount?

HANNUM
You will be able to pursue whatever attracts your imagination next.

TAVERNER
Now we're getting somewhere.

HANNUM
(to Doyle)
This gentleman is the agent who has brought together buyer and seller.

DOYLE
Okay, I've got it.
(to John)
You got it?

JOHN
Quiet.

HANNUM
(To Morash)
Mr. Morash, you have the results of scientific studies to back up your claim.

TAVERNER
He does.

HANNUM
(to Morash)
You understand that I may submit the fragment to my own experts for examination.

TAVERNER
He does.

HANNUM
(To Morash)
And that, if they are not satisfied, I may void the sale.

MORASH
I do.

TAVERNER
No, you don't! A sale is a sale.

HANNUM
Mr. Taverner, I am not buying a watch off your wrist.

TAVERNER
A sale is a sale!

HANNUM
And John knows where you live. Would you rather deal with him?

TAVERNER
Are you threatening me?

HANNUM
Would you like me to?

NOVOTNY
Do what he says, Larry.

TAVERNER
Ten days. You have ten days to consult your experts. Then the deal is final.

HANNUM
Agreed. I was going to propose five days.

TAVERNER
Uh.

HANNUM
I will of course pay you now, Mr. Morash. I know your reputation. I do not expect to have to void the sale.

MORASH
Do you—do you have all that money with you?

HANNUM
In a certified check.

>   *He takes out a thin envelope.*

HANNUM
We can walk to the bank together and negotiate it, if you prefer.

MORASH
No, no. I understand certified checks. I use them all the time.

HANNUM
(to Taverner)
Please take no offence, but I brought your fee in cash. I presumed you would prefer it that way.

>   *He takes out a fat envelope.*

HANNUM
In fifties.

NOVOTNY
Much better that way.

TAVERNER
But how will I get home, with all that cash?

NOVOTNY
I will carry it for you.

DOYLE
And that's just the fee? He gets that just for introducing you to you?

TAVERNER
There's more to it than that.

DOYLE
Like what? No, don't tell me.

HANNUM
Mr. Morash, you of course have the fragment with you?

DOYLE
Wait a minute. If we don't have anything Shakespeare wrote, how would you know *this* isn't something Shakespeare wrote?

Scribbles on napkin; hands napkin to Hannum.

HANNUM
"I wrote this myself: Howdy! Signed, Bill Shakespeare."

DOYLE
There: pay me some big bucks for that.

Andrew Wetmore

HANNUM
Mr. Morash?

MORASH
Well...well, with a piece of writing, there are three categories that I use: likelihood, consonance, and provenance.

DOYLE
Yeah; I'd use those, too.

NOVOTNY
So likelihood would be: would Shakespeare have been likely to write on a napkin?

HANNUM
Yes. And consonance involves asking, did he ever use the word "howdy" in any of his plays or sonnets? Is the message consistent?

MORASH
Exactly. And, er, for provenance, we try to demonstrate who had the fragment ever since it, er, left Shakespeare's hand. And do we have any proof that it existed in the first place?

JOHN
So, like, if somebody wrote in his diary in sixteen something that Bill Shakespeare dropped him a line to say Howdy...

HANNUM
Very good, John. Then we would become very interested in this fragment of Doyle's. Unfortunately...

DOYLE
Okay, give it back. It has sentimental value. He does It's my complete works.

Tucks it into her shirt pocket.

HANNUM
Now, Mr. Morash, does this fragment of yours meet your tests?

MORASH
Likelihood, consonance, and provenance? Oh, yes.

HANNUM
Good.

TAVERNER
Finally!

MORASH
But there may still be a problem.

TAVERNER
There is no problem. You just said.

MORASH
There may still be a problem.

> *From his briefcase, Morash produces a container the size of a cigar box, and a folder of papers, and lays it them the table. Doyle starts to reach for the box, but stops when John puts a hand on her shoulder.*

MORASH
Mr. Hannum, I can vouch absolutely that this is from Shakespeare's hand. I am as sure of this as I am of anything in life. I would lay the whole rest of my collection against it.

TAVERNER
See? then there's no problem.

MORASH
But between you and Taverner and myself, perhaps there has been some confusion.

NOVOTNY
You don't want to sell it?

JOHN
You want more money?

MORASH
I want Mr. Hannum to be happy with his purchase.

TAVERNER
Then sell him the damn thing. Here—

He takes the box. John moves near him.

HANNUM
(to Morash)
Is it safe to open the box?

MORASH
Perfectly safe.

HANNUM
Do not touch the fragment.

TAVERNER
How dumb do you think I am? I'm not going to be the one to mess up this deal. This is a for-sure Shakespeare fragment.

MORASH
It is.

TAVERNER
Not a copy. From his own hand.

MORASH
Yes, but—

TAVERNER
So let's see what the big problem is.

> *Novotny puts a hand on his arm; he shrugs her off.*

TAVERNER
Keep back.
(to Doyle)
You, too.

> *He opens the box and peers inside. Delicately lifts some tissue paper. Then he slowly brings the tissue paper to his mouth, still staring at the box.*

NOVOTNY
Something is wrong?

> *Taverner looks at Morash, and then back into the box.*

NOVOTNY
You are not well?

> *Taverner carefully closes the box and slowly stands up with it. John takes it out of his hands.*

TAVERNER
(to Morash)
I get it. I get it now.

MORASH
Well, as I said—

TAVERNER
You are one sick rich guy. Why can't you collect stamps or coins? Something everybody understands. Something you can sell with no trouble. But no. You have this twisted interest in feathers and who knows what. Did you think this was funny? You want to get me in more trouble than I already got?

MORASH
But you came to me—

TAVERNER
I got good information. The mark wanted a Shakespeare fragment, and you had one you wanted to unload.

MORASH
I am tired of Shakespeare.

TAVERNER
So am I. I am way tired of him now. I am having nothing more to do with him.

> *As he steps away from the table, John takes him by the arm. He shrugs him off.*

TAVERNER
Get off of me!
(to HANNUM)
I didn't have anything to do with this. I was bringing you honest goods. So send your goons after *him*. I quit this deal I wash my hands—I am *really* gonna wash my hands of this.

HANNUM
You are withdrawing?

TAVERNER
Right this minute.
(backing away)
I know what you think of me. But I was brought up right. There are some things I will not do.

NOVOTNY
There are?

TAVERNER
So, just forget it, okay? I'm gone.

NOVOTNY
But what about the money you owe me?

TAVERNER
There's things more important than money!

> *He EXITS UR.*

NOVOTNY
There are not!

> *She starts after him. Comes back to the table.*

NOVOTNY
I am sorry. I should never have been here. I am sorry.

> *She EXITS UR*

DOYLE
(to John)
Well? What's in the box?

JOHN
I don't know.

She crosses to him.

DOYLE
Open it!
(to Hannum)
Is it okay?

HANNUM
Oh, yes.

John opens the box and he and Doyle peer in.

JOHN
I don't get it.

Starts to reach in. Stops.

JOHN
That's...Is that?...

DOYLE
Well, it's a finger bone. Look: there's the knuckle, and there's the—

JOHN
A finger bone?

DOYLE
Didn't you ever see one before? Think of Hallowe'en costumes.

JOHN
I don't get it.

MORASH
It's a simple misunderstanding. I sought this because I wanted it —here are the DNA tests, the record of excavation of the tomb. Once I had it, I grew tired of it. But when people heard I had something from Shakespeare's own hand, they must have thought I meant what he wrote with that hand. Simple mistake, really. But I did not realize it until a few moments ago. I'm afraid I do not think very quickly—

JOHN
Shakespeare's finger? I don't—

> *He sways. Doyle takes the box from his hands.*

DOYLE
What, you never saw one before?

MORASH
And you have?

DOYLE
Working in restaurants, you see all kinds of things.

> *John faints into Doyle's arms.*

DOYLE
Whoa! Easy, there.

> *Doyle and Morash lower John onto the UC table. She loosens his tie.*

MORASH
Is he all right?

DOYLE
It just happens to some people. My uncle Seth is the toughest man I

know, but he cannot give blood. One look at the needle and: powie.

MORASH
I am used to a quieter life.

DOYLE
Then don't go around selling dead men's fingers.

> *She hands the box to him.*

MORASH
A good point.

> *He squares his shoulders.*

MORASH
Mr. Hannum, I am truly sorry for this confusion. Honest mistakes were made on all sides. Perhaps we should leave it at that.

> *Hannum considers the thin envelope, turning it over and over in his hands. Finally he slides it across the table toward Morash.*

HANNUM
Your price is fair for the finger. It is almost unique. I said I would pay it if I am satisfied, and I am.

> *He stands.*

HANNUM
You have, in fact, relieved me of a worry that was tickling my mind: even if one could have a piece of Shakespeare's own writing, how can one be sure it represented the veriest, truest essence of his thought? Every author writes rough copies and revisions and final drafts. And when he thinks he is satisfied, he goes off to the theatre one night and an actor muffs his line and accidentally finds a better

one, and the playwright says, "Oh, wonderful: that's what I was getting at all along!"

But his finger! Who can doubt its connection to his very essence?

> *Morash hands the box to Hannum, and picks up the envelope. Hannum opens the box.*

HANNUM
It is...?

MORASH
The right index finger.

> *He wiggles his own*

HANNUM
Very good.

> *Closes the box.*

HANNUM
How much for the whole hand?

MORASH
What?

HANNUM
As precious as this fragment is, its value will slip if the market is flooded with fingers. "Bard Parts"—I can see it now. How much for the whole hand? Or both hands?

MORASH
Oh, my goodness. I don't know. A whole hand. I would have to consider.

HANNUM
Then we will consider. Without the irritation of third parties. May I invite you to my office?

MORASH
Well…yes, yes.

> *He picks up his briefcase.*

MORASH
But I cannot promise anything.

HANNUM
I don't pay for promises.

> *Morash and Hannum begin to move toward the UR door.*

DOYLE
Yeah, but wait!

> *They stop*

DOYLE
What about your bill? And my tip? And him?

HANNUM
Oh, yes.

> *Inspects John.*

HANNUM
He would be awkward to carry.

> *Extends the fat envelope to Doyle.*

HANNUM
Please secure a taxi for John when he comes around.

DOYLE
I—what? I...all right.

She takes envelope and looks in it.

DOYLE
Sheesh. You want me to *buy* him a taxi?

HANNUM
Part will pay for our refreshments. With the balance I would like to buy your complete works, if they are for sale.

DOYLE
Really?

HANNUM
As long as you discuss these events with no one. Not your colleagues in the kitchen. Not even John.

DOYLE
Done!

Gives him the napkin.

DOYLE
You be sure to come back here when you've got other deals.

HANNUM
What for? You will no longer be here.

DOYLE
(hefting envelope.)
Oh. I guess not.

HANNUM
Ah: I almost forgot.

> *He returns to the DR table, caresses the artificial flower again, and brings his hand away as if holding something.*

MORASH
Ah: A bug! I have been bugged!
(pleased)
This day has been full of new things.

HANNUM
Now to just shut this thing off...

> *He does so.*

HANNUM
And we have a permanent record. In case anybody wants to get deniable at any point in the future.

MORASH
(to Doyle)
It was very nice pie.

DOYLE
Thanks. Nice finger.

> *Hannum and Morash EXIT R.*
> *Doyle inspects the envelope, looks toward the kitchen; starts to call to her colleagues. Looks in the envelope again, and then at John. Tucks the envelope down her front.*

DOYLE
I guess the rest is silence.

                        Blackout
                          END

Shakescenes

Loosely Titus

Time
Now.

Setting
A game show; and, within it, various places in and near classical Rome. Saturninus' camp (M2, W2, M5, M6) is SL, Titus' camp (M3, M4, W1) is SR.

Cast
Six men and two women. W1 and M5 play multiple parts.

M 1: Announcer
M 2: Saturninus, elder son of the late emperor
M 3: Bassianus, younger son of the late emperor
M 4: Titus Andronicus, heroic Roman general
W 1: His children: Lavinia, Lucius, Quintus, Martius, Mutius
W 2: Tamora, the Queen of the Goths
M 5: Her sons: Alarbus, Demetrius, Chiron
M 6: Aaron

The actors, except for the Announcer, have attached to their costumes one or more balloons, representing the lives of the characters they are playing. The actress playing His Children has five balloons, which she either wears all the time or acquires and sets aside according to who she is playing at the time. The actor playing Her Sons has three balloons.

Titus, His Children, and Bassianus all wear tunics or hats of the same colour (the tunic for Titus and the actress playing His Children must have long sleeves); Saturninus, Tamora, Her Sons, and Aaron all wear tunics or hats of a different colour. The Announcer has a network-tv blazer (with T.H.U.S. on the pocket), and wears a headset.

In production, we have found that helium balloons work best. You need a minimum of 34 balloons at the start of the show. It is good to have a reserve supply already inflated, as some inevitably pop or float away while they are still needed. (Famously, the actress playing Titus' children stabbed her own balloon when making a triumphant gesture at the end of the show one night. She just froze in place, with a look of horror on her face.)

Loosely Titus

At rise, the ANNOUNCER is in his broadcast spot.
  Flourish of trumpets.
  The rest of the CAST ENTERS like athletes jogging onto the field, and take their positions in their respective camps.

ANNOUNCER
Hello, and welcome back to the Twenty-four Hour Unlimited Shakespeare Channel—

ALL
(Singing the station theme) "T.H.U.S.: Thus!"

ANNOUNCER
—and to our production of Titus Andronicus, now in progress. And a special welcome to our viewers who have been watching our regional broadcast of Timon of Athens, and now join us; and wasn't that a riveting spectacle.
  Now here's some of the highlights from Andronicus, so you'll know how our hero got himself into his, ahem, titus spotus.

SATURNINUS and BASSIANUS take up speaking poses.

ANNOUNCER
As you remember, the year of the war between Rome and the Goths was also an election year. Saturninus and Bassianus, sons of the late Emperor, were both hoping to be crowned.

They speak at the same time.

SATURNINUS	BASSIANUS
Noble patricians, patrons of my right,	Romans, friends, followers, favourers of my right,
Defend the justice of my cause with arms;	If ever Bassianus, Caesar's son,
And, countrymen, my loving followers,	Were gracious in the eyes of royal Rome,
Plead my successive title with your swords.	Keep then this passage to the Capitol.
I am his firstborn that was the last	And suffer not dishonour to approach,
That ware the imperial diadem of Rome.	The imperial seat, to virtue consecrate,
Then let my father's honours live in me,	To justice, continence, and nobility;
Nor wrong mine age with this indignity.	But let desert in pure election shine,
And, Romans, fight for freedom in your choice.	And, Romans, fight for freedom in your choice.

Applause.

ANNOUNCER
The vote count was a dead heat. And in the best tradition of one man, one vote, the election was in the hands of Titus Andronicus, the greatest general in the war.

Titus takes up a position between them.

ANNOUNCER
You've got to hand it to Titus: not only did he interrupt a promising career in the Senate to go off to war, he took his twenty-five sons with him.

Titus displays 21 balloons besides his own; His Children flourish 5.

ANNOUNCER
And the Goths killed 21 of them.

Tamora, Aaron, and Tamora's Sons pop the 21 balloons Titus holds.

ANNOUNCER
After that twenty-one son salute, Titus won the war with the help of his four surviving sons, Lucius, Quintus, Martius, and Mutius.

His Children takes a different heroic pose for each son.

ANNOUNCER
He even captured Tamora, the Queen of the Goths, her three sons Alarbus, Chiron, and Demetrius,

Her Sons takes a different heroic pose for each son.

ANNOUNCER
And Aaron, her nasty counsellor.

Aaron makes a rude gesture, as with bound hands.

ANNOUNCER
He brought them to Rome in chains.

HIS CHILDREN
(as Lucius)
Father, give us a prisoner of the Goths,
That we may hew his limbs, and on a pile
Ad manes fratrum sacrifice his flesh
Before this earthy prison of their bones,
That so the shadows be not unappeased,
Nor we disturbed with prodigies on earth.

Titus takes a balloon from Her Sons and gives it to His Children.

Andrew Wetmore

TITUS
I give him you, the noblest that survives.
The eldest son of this distressèd queen.

LUCIUS
Away with him! And make a fire straight,
And, with our swords, upon a pile of wood,
Let's hew his limbs till they be clean consumed.

Pops the balloon. Her Sons reacts.

TAMORA
O cruel, irreligious piety!

ANNOUNCER
Then Titus cast his vote. Sources close to Andronicus tell me he had already promised his daughter Lavinia to Bassianus. So to keep peace in Rome, he chose for emperor the older brother, Saturninus.

BASSIANUS
He what?

Bassianus is deflated.
Titus crowns Her Sons.
All cheer.

SATURNINUS
Titus Andronicus, for thy favors done
I give thee thanks in part of thy deserts,
And will with deeds requite thy gentleness.
And, for an onset, Titus, to advance
Thy name and honorable family,
Lavinia will I make my empress.

He seizes His Children.

BASSIANUS
No fair!

TITUS
He is the emperor.

HIS CHILDREN
(As Livinia)
But—

TITUS
(to Tamora)
Now, madam, are you prisoner to an emperor,
To him that for your honor and your state
Will use you nobly and your followers.

SATURNINUS
(to the audience)
Woah! A goodly lady, of the hue
That I would choose, were I to choose anew.
(to Tamora)
Clear up, fair Queen, that cloudy countenance.
Princely shall be your usage...
(leering)
every way.
Rest on my word, and I will comfort you.

Bassianus seizes His Children.

BASSIANUS
Lord Titus, by your leave, this maid is mine.

TITUS
Traitors avaunt! Where is the Emperor's guard?
Treason, my lord! Lavinia is surprised.

Andrew Wetmore

SATURNINUS
Surprised? By whom?

BASSIANUS
By him that justly may
Bear his betrothed from all the world away.

TITUS
Traitor! Restore Lavinia to the Emperor!

> *Titus grabs for them. They dodge. He pops one of His Children's balloons.*

ANNOUNCER
Oh, that's an unlucky break. Titus just killed his own son—I think it's Mutius; I can't see the number on his jersey. Yes, it's Mutius. Mutiulated. Oh my, oh my.

TITUS
The dismal'st day is this that e'er I saw,
To be dishonored by my sons in Rome!
Well, bury him—and Bassianus next.

> *He starts again for Bassianus.*

SATURNINUS
No, Titus, no.

> *Titus stops.*

SATURNINUS
The Emperor needs her not,
Nor her, nor thee, nor any of thy stock.
I'll trust by leisure him that mocks me once;
Thee never, nor thy traitorous haughty sons,

Confederates all thus to dishonor me.

TITUS
O monstrous! What reproachful words are these?

SATURNINUS
And therefore, lovely Tamora, Queen of the Goths,
If thou be pleased with this my sudden choice,
Behold, I choose thee, Tamora, for my bride,
And will create thee Empress of Rome.

Cheers, boos, cries of confusion.

ANNOUNCER
Well, will you look at that! The Queen of the Goths has taken advantage of Lavinia's absence, and seems to have snatched victory out of the jaws of defeat!

TITUS
I am not bid to wait upon this bride.
Titus, when wert thou wont to walk alone,
Dishonored thus, and challengèd of wrongs?

HIS CHILDREN
(as Livinia)
My lord, to step out of these dreary dumps,
How comes it that the subtle Queen of Goths
Is of a sudden thus advanced in Rome?

SATURNINUS
(to Bassianus)
Traitor, if Rome have law or we have power
Thou and thy faction shall repent this rape.

BASSIANUS
"Rape" call you it, my lord, to seize my own,

My true-betrothèd love and now my wife?

SATURNINUS
'Tis good, sir. You are very short with us,
But if we live we'll be as sharp with you.

> *He threatens Bassianus. Titus steps between them and threatens Saturninus. Tamora catches Saturninus' arm. Her Sons and Aaron support Saturninus. His Children support Bassianus. There is a shoving match; Titus slips to one knee.*

ANNOUNCER
And we may have a bench-clearing brawl here.

TAMORA
My worthy lord...

> *All freeze.*

TAMORA
...if ever Tamora
Were gracious in those princely eyes of thine,
Then hear me speak indifferently for all;
And at my suit, sweet, pardon what is past.

SATURNINUS
What, madam? Be dishonored openly,
And basely put it up without revenge?

TAMORA
Come, come, sweet Emperor. Come, Andronicus.
Take up this good old man, and cheer the heart
That dies in tempest of thy angry frown.

SATURNINUS
Rise, Titus, rise. My empress hath prevailed.

Titus rises. Everyone else stands down.

ANNOUNCER
A perfect, peacemaking performance by the newly-noble lady.

TITUS
I thank your Majesty, and her, my lord.
These words, these looks, infuse new life in me.

TAMORA
Titus, I am incorporate in Rome,
A Roman now adopted happily,
And must advise the Emperor for his good.
This day all quarrels die, Andronicus.

He kisses her hand; then, as he turns away, she kicks him so he reels forward and knocks down Aaron, who knocks down Her Sons.

ANNOUNCER
Oh, my goodness! Oh, my goodness! Let's run that back: we've got to have another look at that.

All move backward to their position when Titus kissed Tamora's hand, and then go through the sequence again in slow motion as the Announcer talks.

ANNOUNCER
Now that's one for the highlight films! There's Tamora, the girl who has everything—Queen of the Goths, Empress of Rome—and in the middle of patching up a feud that could split the Empire, she stoops to unnecessary roughness. Oh, my goodness. The commissioner is going to have to take a close look at this one. And this could be trouble, too: Titus has clobbered Aaron, the Queen's hit-man, who was standing out-of-bounds. Really cleaned his clock.

Andrew Wetmore

Titus couldn't help it, but Aaron is not the sort of guy you can do that to. I thought we were in danger of a happy ending there for a minute...but you never know what will happen next on the Twenty-four Hour Unlimited Shakespeare Channel!

ALL
(singing)
"T.H.U.S.: Thus!"

> *The two parties retreat to their camps, except for Aaron and Her Sons.*

AARON
I'll find a day to massacre them all
And raze their faction and their family,
The cruel father and his traitorous sons,

HER SONS
And Bassianus, and Lavinia.

AARON
...Lavinia.

HER SONS
Aaron, a thousand deaths
Would I propose to achieve her whom I love.

AARON
To achieve her? How?

HER SONS
Why makes thou it so strange?
She is a woman, therefore may be wooed;
She is a woman, therefore may be won;
She is Lavinia, therefore must be loved.
What, man, more water glideth by the mill

Than knows the miller of, and easy it is
Of a cut loaf to steal a slice, we know.
Though Bassianus be the Emperor's brother,
Better than he have worn the cuckold's badge.

AARON
The Emperor's court is like a house of Fame,
The palace full of tongues, of eyes, and ears;
The woods are ruthless, dreadful, deaf, and dull.
There speak and strike, brave boys, and take your turns;
There serve your lust, shadowed from heaven's eye,
And revel in Lavinia's treasury.

HER SONS
Thy counsel, lad, smells of no cowardice.

> *Her Sons lie in wait for Bassianus and Lavinia, who are promenading. As they pass, the SONS detach Bassianus' balloon. When he and Lavinia have gone a little distance:*

HER SONS
Good day, my lord and lady!

> *Bassianus turns and waves grandly. Her Sons pop the balloon. Bassianus reacts and dies, DL.*
>   *Lavinia turns to flee, but Aaron is on one side of her, Tamora is upstage of her.*

TAMORA
Give me the poniard. You shall know, my boys,
Your mother's hand shall right your mother's wrong.

HER SONS
Stay, madam, here is more belongs to her.
First thresh the corn, then after burn the straw.

Andrew Wetmore

TAMORA
But when ye have the honey ye desire,
Let not this wasp outlive, us both to sting.

>*She goes back to her camp.*

HER SONS
I warrant you madam, we will make that sure.

>*They muss His Children's hair, kick her butt, pull her nose, and disfigure her balloon; then cut off her hands and pull out her tongue, as the Announcer speaks.*

ANNOUNCER
Where are the officials when you need them? Look at how they're treating her! Ooh, what disrespect. She would be better off dead. This is a very tough league, and they play for keeps.
   And what now? Oh, yes, it looks like the old Tereus and Philomela play. Yes, that's it—they're going to let her live to shame her father Andronicus, but they're pulling out her tongue and cutting off her hands, so she won't be able to say who did it. There's one hand...and there's the other. Oh, that's gotta hurt.

>*Her Sons swagger back to their camp, while His Children gesticulates and mouths her grief.*

ANNOUNCER
Yes, I think she's going to find it very difficult to do her song now.

>*As His Children staggers back to her camp, Aaron collects Bassianus's balloon, crosses to Bassianus's body, then signals to His Children (as two of Titus' sons). They come forward; he hands them the balloon, then runs to Saturninus.*

ANNOUNCER
And now Aaron has lured two more of Titus' sons to the place where Bassianus lies. Could he be trying for a triple play?

His Children look at the corpse, finger the balloon.

HIS CHILDREN
(as one of his sons)
Lord Bassianus lies berayed in blood,
All on a heap, like to a slaughtered lamb,
In this detested, dark, blood-drinking pit.
Upon his bloody finger he doth wear
A precious ring that lightens all this hole,
Which like a taper in some monument
Doth shine upon the dead man's earthy cheeks.

Saturninus, Tamora, Her Sons, and Aaron arrive. Titus comes forward to observe.

SATURNINUS
Along with me! I'll see what hole is here,
And what he is that now is leapt into it.
Say, who art thou that lately didst descend
Into this gaping hollow of the earth?

HIS SONS
(as one of his sons)
The unhappy sons of old Andronicus,
Brought hither in a most unlucky hour
To find thy brother Bassianus dead.

They gesture with the balloon, then realize what they're doing and try to hide it.

HIS CHILDREN
Oops.

Andrew Wetmore

SATURNINUS
(to TITUS)
Two of thy whelps, fell curs of bloody kind,
Have here bereft my brother of his life!

HIS CHILDREN
(as one of his sons)
But—

SATURNINUS
Sirs, drag them from the pit unto the prison!

> *Her Sons take two of His Children's balloons and conceal them, then return to their camp. The His Children actress becomes Lucius.*

SATURNINUS
There let them bide until we have devised
 Some never-heard-of torturing pain for them.

> *Saturninus' party returns to their camp.*

ANNOUNCER
Now Titus has two boys in the penalty box, and only Lavinia and Lucius for comfort. There's nobody left on the bench, and that could be decisive in the late innings.

TITUS
Ah, Lucius, for thy brothers let me plead.
Grave tribunes, once more I entreat of you—

HIS CHILDREN
(as Lucius)
My gracious lord, no tribune hears you speak.

TITUS
Why, 'tis no matter, man. If they did hear,
They would not mark me; if they did mark,
They would not pity me; yet plead I must.
And bootless unto them,
Therefore I tell my sorrows to the stones.
When I do weep, they humbly at my feet
Receive my tears and seem to weep with me.
A stone is soft as wax, tribunes more hard than stones,
A stone is silent and offendeth not,
And tribunes with their tongues doom men to death.
But wherefore stand'st thou with thy weapon drawn?

LUCIUS
To rescue my two brothers from their death,
For which attempt the judges have pronounced
My everlasting doom of banishment.

TITUS
O happy man! They have befriended thee.
Why, foolish Lucius, dost thou not perceive
That Rome is but a wilderness of tigers?
Tigers must prey, and Rome affords no prey
But me and mine. How happy art thou then
From these devourers to be banishèd!

AARON
(approaching)
Titus Andronicus, my lord the Emperor
Sends thee this word: that if thou love thy sons,
Chop off your hand and send it to the King.
He for the same will send thee both thy sons
And that shall be the ransom for their fault.

Andrew Wetmore

TITUS
O gracious Emperor! O gentle Aaron!
With all my heart I'll send the King my hand.
Lend me thy hand, and I will give thee mine.

> *Aaron cuts off his hand, then produces two withered balloons.*

AARON
Foolish Andronicus, ill art thou repaid
For that good hand thou sent'st the Emperor.
Here are the heads of thy two noble sons.
And here's thy hand in scorn to thee sent back—sucker.

> *He returns to his camp.*

ANNOUNCER
You know, I can't believe Saturninus knew about this. I wonder who could be behind it. My goodness, I can't think how the Andronici will recover from this one.

TITUS
Why, I have not another tear to shed.
Besides, this sorrow is an enemy,
And would usurp upon my watery eyes
And make them blind with tributary tears.
Then which way shall I find Revenge's cave?
For these two heads do seem to speak to me,
And threat me I shall never come to bliss
Till all these mischiefs be returned again
Even in their throats that have committed them.
Lucius, boy, go get thee from my sight;
Thou art an exile, and thou must not stay.
Hie to the Goths and raise an army there.
And if ye love me, as I think you do,
Let's kiss and part, for we have much to do.

HIS CHILDREN
(as Lucius)
Farewell, Andronicus, my noble father,
The woefull'st man that ever lived in Rome.
Now will I to the Goths and raise a power
to be revenged on Rome and Saturnine.

Goes to Titus' camp, changes to Lavinia.

ANNOUNCER
So Titus is going to try the raise-the-Goths gambit, a desperate measure. Tamora is the queen of the Goths. While they love her, they'll never follow Lucius. I'm afraid it's all over for the Andronicus team.

TITUS
And, Lavinia, thou shalt be employed:

His Children, as Lavinia, crosses eagerly to Titus.

TITUS
Bear thou my hand, sweet wench, between thy teeth.
Thou hast no hands to wipe away thy tears,
 Nor tongue to tell me who hath martyred thee.

His Children uses semaphore to spell out "Tamora's sons."

TITUS
T...Ta...Timor?...Tom Morrison?...
"Tamora's sons"! Ah, me!
I had forgot thou hadst a merit badge
In signalling.
Tamora's sons did this?
O ruler of the mighty heavens, are you so slow
To see and hear the crimes that are committed?

Andrew Wetmore

Well, we will prosecute by good advice
Mortal revenge upon these traitorous Goths
And see their blood, or die with this reproach.

> *The return to their camp.*
> *Saturninus and his followers take centre stage.*

HER SONS
Arms, my king! Rome never had more cause.
The Goths have gathered head, and with a power
Of high-resolvèd men bent to the spoil
They hither march amain under conduct
Of Lucius, son to old Andronicus.

SATURNINUS
Is warlike Lucius general of the Goths?

ANNOUNCER
They must have found out that Tamora was spending far too much time in the huddle with her servant Aaron.

> *Tamora hands Aaron a baby-shaped bundle.*

AARON
Look how the young slave smiles upon the father,
As who should say, "Old lad, I am thy own."

> *Tamora shushes him. He EXITS with the baby.*

ANNOUNCER
A tactical error for the Queen: say what you will about the Goths, they really believe in traditional family values. They don't like their queens getting caught with their hand in the nooky jar. My, my. This mistake has set the Queen's own people against her. But will they be able to overcome the might Rome? I think so.

TAMORA
(to Announcer)
You: shut up!

SATURNINUS
These tidings nip me, and I hang the head
As flowers with frost or grass beat down with storms.
Ay, now begins our sorrows to approach.

TAMORA
Why should you fear? Is not your city strong?

SATURNINUS
Ay, but the citizens favor Lucius,
And will revolt from me to succor him.

TAMORA
O, cheer thy spirit, for know, thou Emperor,
I will enchant the old Andronicus
With words more sweet and yet more dangerous
Than baits to fish or honey-stalks to sheep,
For I can smooth and fill his agèd ears
With golden promises, that were his heart
Almost impregnable, his old ears deaf,
Yet should both ear and heart obey my tongue.

ANNOUNCER
I think it's going to go down to the final moments of play. Tamora has somehow blown a commanding lead. Titus is down to one son and some fragments of a daughter, but he just won't give up. What a competitor!

> *Tamora and Her Sons, disguised, approach the Andronicus camp and knock.*

Andrew Wetmore

TITUS
Who doth molest my contemplation?

TAMORA
If thou didst know me, thou wouldst talk with me.

TITUS
I am not mad; I know thee well enough.
Witness this wretched stump, these lines of grief and care.
Witness the tiring day and heavy night,
Witness all sorrow, that I know thee well
For our proud empress, mighty Tamora.
Is not thy coming for my other hand?

TAMORA
Know, thou sad man, I am not Tamora;
She is thy enemy, and I thy friend.
I am Revenge, sent from th'infernal kingdom
To ease the gnawing vulture of thy mind
By working wreakful vengeance on thy foes.

TITUS
And who are they beside thee?

TAMORA
These are my ministers, and come with me.
Rape and Murder, they are callèd so
'Cause they take vengeance of such kind of men.
(to the audience)
This closing with him fits his lunacy.
For now he firmly takes me for Revenge;
And, being credulous in this mad thought,
I'll make him send for Lucius his son,
And whilst I at a banquet hold him sure,
I'll find some cunning practice out of hand
To scatter and disperse the giddy Goths

Or at the least make them his enemies.

TITUS
(as if it is his own idea)
I'll send for Lucius, my thrice-valiant son,
Who leads towards Rome a band of warlike Goths,
And bid him come and banquet at my house.

TAMORA
I will bring in the Empress and her sons,
The Emperor himself, and all thy foes,
And at thy mercy shall they stoop and kneel,
And on them shalt thou ease thy angry heart.
What says Andronicus to this device?

TITUS
Neat! They won't suspect a thing.

Tamora goes to collect the emperor.

TITUS
(to Her Sons)
What a good idea.

He laughs. Her Sons start to laugh with him. When they double over laughing, Titus seizes their balloons.

TITUS
So: one is Murder and Rape is the other's name.
Therefore I bind them: no more threaten us.
Oft have I cried to heaven for such an hour,
And now I find it.

HER SONS
Titus, forbear! We are the Empress's sons!

Andrew Wetmore

TITUS
O villains, braggarts, bullies, murderers!
Here stands the spring whom you have stained with mud,
This goodly summer with your winter mixed.
You killed her husband, and for that vile fault
Two of her brothers were condemned to death.
Villains, for shame. You could not beg for grace.
You know your mother means to feast with me,
And calls herself Revenge, and thinks me mad.
At that feast, and in that character
I shall return the children to their dam.

He pops the balloons. Her Sons die DR.
Titus and His Children set a table with a preset feast.

ANNOUNCER
And the offspring standings are Andronicus 24 and a half
deceased, Tamora three. That's a new scoring record for a live
broadcast—and there's more to come! Like Yogi Berra used to say,
it's never over 'til the Dark Lady sings.

Saturninus, Aaron, and Tamora approach the table.

TITUS
Welcome, my gracious lord; welcome dread Queen;
Welcome, with warlike Goths, my Lucius;
And welcome, all. Although the cheer be poor,
'Twill fill your stomachs. Please you eat of it.

TAMORA
(nibbling)
Mmm—We are beholding to you, good Andronicus.

TITUS
An if your Highness knew my heart, you were.
My lord the Emperor, resolve me this:

Was it well done of the fellow in the tale
To slay his daughter with his own right hand
Because she was enforced, stained, and deflowered?

SATURNINUS
It was, Andronicus.

TITUS
Your reason, mighty lord?

SATURNINUS
Because the girl should not survive her shame,
And by her presence still renew his sorrows.

TITUS
A reason mighty, and effectual—more mustard?
A pattern, precedent, and lively warrant
For me, most wretched, to perform the like.
Die, die, Lavinia, [LAVINIA squeaks in protest]
and thy shame with thee,
And with thy shame thy father's sorrow die.

Pops Lavinia's balloon. She dies. His Children becomes Lucius.

ANNOUNCER
That's one for the books.

TAMORA
Why has thou slain thine only daughter thus?

TITUS
Not I: your sons are they who did her in.
They ravished her and cut away her tongue,
And they, 'twas they that did her all this wrong.

SATURNINUS
(to Aaron)
Go fetch them hither to us presently.

    Aaron EXITS.

TITUS
Why, there they are, both bakèd in this pie,
Whereof their mother daintily hath fed,

    Tamora pulls a popped balloon out of her mouth.

TITUS
Eating the flesh that she herself hath bred.
'Tis true, 'tis true; witness my knife's sharp point.

    He pops Tamora's balloon. She dies.

SATURNINUS
Die, frantic wretch, for this accursèd deed!

    He pops Titus' balloon. He dies.

HIS CHILDREN
(as Lucius)
Can the son's eye behold his father bleed?
There's meed for meed, death for a deadly deed!

    Uses the crown to pop Saturninus' balloon. He dies.
    His Children put on the crown.

ANNOUNCER
What a turnaround! What an upset! A lollapaloser of a finish Lucius just came out of nowhere to win that final round. Yow! Let's go have a word with Lucius Andronicus, the new Emperor of Rome.

Announcer crosses to His Children.
Aaron ENTERS, inspects the corpses in confusion.

ANNOUNCER
Lucius, what was it that inspired you to—

HIS CHILDREN
(as Lucius)
As for that ravenous tiger, Tamora,
No funeral rite nor quiet grave for her.
But throw her forth to beasts and birds of prey.
(to Announcer)
And as for you—

ANNOUNCER
(retreating)
You sad Andronicus, have done with woes.

Announcer grabs Aaron.

ANNOUNCER
Give sentence on this execrable wretch,
That hath been breeder of these dire events.

AARON
Not me! Have mercy! I'm a single parent!

Announcer secures Aaron's balloon and presents it to His Children.

HIS CHILDREN
(as Lucius)
Set him breast-deep in earth and famish him:
There let him stand and rave and cry for food.
If anyone relieves or pities him,

Andrew Wetmore

For the offence he dies. This is our doom.

AARON
Ah, why should wrath be mute and fury dumb?
I am no baby, I, that with base prayers
I should repent the evils I have done.
Ten thousand worse than ever yet I did
Would I perform, if I might have my will.
If one good deed in all my life I did,
I do repent it from my very soul.

> *His Children gradually lets the air out of Aaron's balloon during this speech, and he slowly sinks to his death.*
> *His Children assume a heroic pose.*

ANNOUNCER
I'm afraid Lucius Andronicus is too busy with affairs of state for an interview. The final tally for Titus Andronicus tonight: 33 onstage deaths, three hands cut off, and a really interesting cooking lesson.
   And that's all the time we have. Thank you for being with us, and please stay tuned for the Broad Street Pantomime Theatre presentation of all 153 of Shakespeare's sonnets. It's always much ado about something, here on the Twenty-four Hour Unlimited Shakespeare Channel.

ALL
(singing)
"T.H.U.S.: Thus!"

> *Flourish of trumpets.*

BLACKOUT
END

Shakescenes

Andrew Wetmore

Acknowledgements

Many, many actors have put time, insights, and effort into performing theses plays in workshops and readings, helping me to get them to their current state. Producers and directors have taken chances that one of my scripts would work for their group (and have generally been rewarded).

In particular I would like to thank the leadership of Hampshire Shakespeare Company in Amherst, Massachusetts; Boston's Playwrights' Platform; Merrimack Valley Playwrights (MVP) in Lowell, Massachusetts; and the Script Happens program at the Saint John Theatre in New Brunswick.

Thank you to Brenda Thompson and Moose House Publications for giving my scripts a chance to find new readers and, possibly, productions.

The author as Titus in a Ghostlight Theater production of "Titus Andronicus" in New Hampshire. Great research opportunity, and worth the loss of a hand.

About the author

Andrew Wetmore trained as a performer, but concluded relatively early that his skills did not match his enthusiasm in a way that would support a professional acting career. Instead, he has spent decades working with community theatres and regional playwrights. He was the founding chairperson of Dramatists' Co-op, an initiative by the Writers' Federation of Nova Scotia to improve the quality and increase the visibility of Nova Scotia-written scripts. For many years he was artistic director of Moveable Feast Theater, which performed in Quebec and Massachusetts. He founded and coordinated MVP (Merrimack Valley Playwrights), where writers in northern Massachusetts could hear their scripts read by trained actors and get constructive feedback on them from their writing and acting colleagues.

Wetmore was born in Nova Scotia, and has returned to the province after many years 'down the road.' He is the editor for Moose House Publications, and for the infrastructure team of the Apache Software Foundation.

www.ingramcontent.com/pod-product-compliance
Lightning Source LLC
Chambersburg PA
CBHW071418070526
44578CB00003B/596